UNIVERSITY OF NORTH CAROLINA
STUDIES IN THE ROMANCE LANGUAGES AND LITERATURES
Number 51

SOCIAL DRAMA
IN NINETEENTH-CENTURY SPAIN

SOCIAL DRAMA
IN NINETEENTH-CENTURY SPAIN

BY

J. HUNTER PEAK

CHAPEL HILL
THE UNIVERSITY OF NORTH CAROLINA PRESS

DEPÓSITO LEGAL: 2.068 — 1964
ARTES GRÁFICAS SOLER, S. A. — VALENCIA — 1964

CONTENTS

	Page
INTRODUCTION	11

CHAPTER

		Page
I.	BEGINNINGS	15
II.	CONTINUATORS OF THE MORATÍN TRADITION	30
III.	TRUTH AND COMMON SENSE	46
IV.	ECHEGARAY—ROMANTICISM IN REALISM	71
V.	MINOR PLAYWRIGHTS	81
VI.	DICENTA AND GALDÓS	106
VII.	CONCLUSIONS	140
BIBLIOGRAPHY		167

DEDICATION

To Sturgis E. Leavitt, counselor and friend, without whose generosity, patience, and constant encouragement, this study would never have been completed.

INTRODUCTION

In Spain the first writer of plays with a moral purpose was not closely allied with the dramatic beginnings of the nineteenth century. Rather, the thread may be traced back through the Age of Classicism and Neo-Classicism of the eighteenth century to the great *dramaturgos* of the *Siglo de Oro* and to Juan Ruiz de Alarcón (1581-1639), who was born in Mexico, but lived most of his life in Spain. The factor differentiating his greatest plays from those of the other leading playwrights of his time is his determined purpose to teach and even to present something of a thesis in such *comedias* as *La verdad sospechosa*, *Las paredes oyen*, and *El examen de maridos*.

In the first named and perhaps the best play, *La verdad sospechosa*, Alarcón makes a plea for honesty by causing the truth to be suspect. Of course, *La verdad sospechosa* is essentially a play written to entertain, but a moral purpose is contained therein. *Las paredes oyen* is the complement of *La verdad sospechosa*. It is a critical study of slander, a eulogy of honesty. There is a lesson to be learned from the development of the plot, and some light sermonizing is provided for the audience who may have missed the point. *El examen de maridos* constitutes a charming study of manners (much like the *comedia de costumbres* so popular just two hundred years afterward); its plot, both clear and original, is devised to reveal the unselfishness of friendship.

Though this obvious concern with ethics is more pronounced in the plays of Alarcón than in those of other Golden Age dramatists, ideas of social justice appear frequently among the plots created by Lope de Vega, such as in *Peribáñez o el comendador de Ocaña* and *El mejor alcalde el rey*. In these an effective solution to problems of oppression by persons in authority is brought about by the appearance of the king, in a *deus ex machina* surprise ending. There is no thesis here, and Lope is not beset with social implications, and yet he is presenting a situation that demands a remedy.

There were yet other playwrights who wrote in similar vein during this period. Rojas Zorrilla, like Alarcón, wrote at least two exceptional plays with an ethical purpose, notably: *Del rey abajo ninguno* and *Entre bobos anda el juego*. And at the end of the Golden Age Moreto delighted the Madrid audience with his *El desdén con el desdén* and *El lindo don Diego*, in each of which one of the leading characters is taught a well-deserved lesson.

In the eighteenth century the plays of Calderón and his imitators and some of the works of Tirso de Molina and Lope continued to be presented, but little originality appeared in the national theater. But, well after the middle of the century, a new influence was felt in dramatic production. In 1774 Gaspar Melchor de Jovellanos, statesman, economist, educator, and poet, reflecting this influence of French drama, presented at Aranjuez in the very presence of the monarch (Charles III), whose severe laws affecting duels it clearly criticized, *El delincuente honrado*. A five-act *comedia llorona*, the Spanish counterpart of the French *drame bourgeois*, it is the model of a type which had a fair vogue in Spain. Only a mediocre play, it is, nevertheless, important because it is one of the few Spanish dramatic works in which the reader or spectator may catch a faint glimpse of the moral and philosophic preoccupations of the eighteenth century. Above all, it remains today one of the most readable dramas of the neo-classic school. Less objective, less realistic, but more purposeful than either Tomás de Iriarte or Moratín the younger, Jovellanos joins them in pointing the way to the comedy of manners that was to develop in the nineteenth century. Indeed, he was among the first to attempt the thesis play by discussing in *El delincuente honrado* social problems of his time. In this play his purpose was to inveigh against the cruelty of the law which meted out the death penalty to all duelists, to both challenger and the challenged.

Tomás de Iriarte wrote two classic comedies, *El señorito mimado* (1788) and *La señorita mal-criada* (1788-1791), in which he "fustiga los defectos de la educación", and proves himself to be the real precursor of Moratín the younger, whose works represent the best achievement of the classic comedies in Spain.

As might be surmised from the title, *El señorito mimado o la mala educación*, a three-act comedy in verse, is a humorous account of a "spoiled brat's" being taught a deserved lesson. Because of his extensive *calaveradas* he loses his *novia* to a more acceptable rival. The plot is slight, the interest in the play depending on comic characters and dialogue. The moral lesson —a well-meaning attack against too indulgent mothers, hence against inadequate or faulty education practices— is effectively presented through the action of the play, and is frequently given emphasis by the *razonamientos* of Cristóbal, the uncle and guardian of the rake so fittingly described in the title.

La señorita mal-criada is the feminine counterpart of its predecessor. Whereas the *señorito mimado* was too actively engaged in the vicious pursuits open to men, Pepita, the *señorita mal-criada*, is not wayward, but childish, capricious, willful, and at times maliciously contrary. In the final scenes she is taught her lesson when the eligible bachelor who had courted her with honorable intentions refuses her offer of marriage.

Within the plot of several of the plays mentioned are the seeds of the comedy of manners and social drama. The first of the nineteenth-century Spanish playwrights to write acceptable plays of this type was Moratín. Though a reasonably popular dramatist in his own day, his importance in the history of Spanish literature is that he was the writer who best represents the transition between the neo-classic drama of the eighteenth century and the drama of the nineteenth century up to the Romantic period (1830's-1840's). It is with his plays that we begin our study of nineteenth-century social drama.

CHAPTER I

BEGINNINGS

Leandro Fernández de Moratín (1760-1828) tried his literary wings in various genres, including epic poetry, *La toma de Granada;* literary satire, *La derrota de los pedantes;* translations such as *Hamlet* and plays by Molière; and, a work of erudition, *Los orígenes del teatro español,* still consulted for its exact and rare information.

But whatever the merits of the works mentioned above, Moratín's fame rests principally on his dramatic work. His doctrine can be studied in the productions mentioned above, in the *Comedia nueva* and in the *Discurso preliminar* to the 1825 edition of his works. At first glance it seems to represent a narrow rigid classicism. But in the author's practice this became notably attenuated and modified. Although the two essential characteristics of his theater, skilled observation of the human heart and a moral aim, place him on a higher level than most contemporary authors, and, although in philosophic values as well as in qualities of simplicity, clearness and wise planning, his plays show his indebtedness to the study of French writers, yet Moratín remains Spanish in subjects, characters and conscientious observation of the society about him. His comedy, in his own words, "wears *basquiña* and *mantilla*". He is quick to recognize that the best rules in the world cannot make up for lack of genius or at least of talent, and therefore he esteems and respects the masters of the Golden Age, even when he deems their ways mistaken. Moratín's real merit lies in the fact that he discovered the right proportion in which to mix the pseudoclassic rules, in so far as they are sound and just, with the legitimate traditions of native taste. He succeeded better than any of his predecessors in blending the two systems and pleasing both intellectuals and the *mosqueteros*. Although the central thought of each of his comedies is simple and logical, the plot is, in general, rich in byplay and sudden turns and ingenious in its picturesque and diverting details. Menéndez y Pelayo says that, "en cuanto a la exactitud y casi la perfección de la lengua castellana, Moratín es uno de los escritores más eminentes de nuestro idioma o de cualquier otro".

El viejo y la niña, the earliest of Moratín's plays, was presented in the Teatro del Príncipe in Madrid, May 22, 1790, but it was written in 1786 or before. Such a provocative subject as a *setentón* marrying a nineteen-year-old would indicate that a marriage of this kind was not unusual in the last years of the eighteenth century and that Moratín felt strongly about it. But playwriting to correct weaknesses in the social structure was new in Spain, and it is not surprising that Moratín encountered difficulties in having the play staged.

In 1786 when the author read *El viejo y la niña* to the dramatic group of a Manuel Martínez, the actors recognized it as a promising vehicle, but feared the audience's reaction to a play which was an attack on a social problem. It was almost unheard of to present a play for any reason other than for entertainment. To further complicate the matter, a misunderstanding with an aging *dama* who wanted to play the part of the youthful Isabel caused Moratín to relinquish, for the time being at least, his intentions of presenting *El viejo y la niña*, now weakened by the many changes demanded by the company and the censor.

Two years later Moratín decided to restore his play to something like its original form. He offered it to the Eusebio Ribera company, had similar difficulties with another "experienced" actress, and, what is more, was refused a *licencia* to stage it by the ecclesiastical authority. Finally, in 1790, *El viejo y la niña* was presented *con aplauso*. It was the beginning of Leandro Fernández de Moratín's successful dramatic career. In addition to its local success, we are told that soon afterward a translation of the play was presented with acclaim in Italy. But many *primeras damas* found the work too austere and melancholy; and with subsequent changes demanded by them, *El viejo y la niña*, "faltando a la verosimilitud, incurrió en una contradicción de principios tan manifiesta, que no tiene disculpa".[1]

What is the play like? It is written in three acts, in verse, and is clearly a play with a thesis. Though Moratín had a moral lesson to put across, El viejo y la niña contains most of the elements of good drama. Moratín appeared on the Spanish dramatic scene at a time when the revival of classic or neo-classic drama was popular in certain quarters. He was influenced by the current demand for observance of the unities, and without obvious effort the author notably succeeded in observing all three in El viejo y la niña. The action begins sometime in the morning of a certain day and concludes before noon of the same day. All the action takes place within the house of don Roque.

In this play the influence of Molière is apparent, especially in the characterization, which is skillfully drawn and carefully delineated. The technical conventions of the day seem to have been well observed, and, from this point of view, Moratín's play must have pleased his contemporaries.

In El viejo y la niña don Roque, a setentón, has recently married Isabel, a girl of nineteen, who at her father's death had been left in the tender care of a tutor (who never appears). To further his own selfish interests, the tutor has persuaded Isabel of the advisability of marrying Roque, a close friend of her father's. The plot of the play is developed from a chance visit to the new household by Isabel's former and only sweetheart, Juan. Juan's jealousies, and the fears and mingled emotions occasioned by her conversation with him combine to make Isabel realize that her marriage with Roque cannot and, for reasons of morality and for the preservation of her own sanity, must not continue. The only escape open to a respectable girl was to enter a convent, which Isabel determines to do at the end of the play.

Clearly enough, the author's purpose is to show the tragic consequences which usually follow such an unhappy union. Moratín's thesis is that a girl should not be taught such blind obedience that it extends to marriage against her will. On several occasions the author has Muñoz, Roque's servant, Isabel, and —at the end

---

[1] PASCUAL HERNÁNDEZ, Comedias de Moratín, Paris, 1881, p. 3.

of the play, now cognizant of his offense against society— Roque himself, expound on this thesis and the tragic consequences to be expected when people of such difference in age marry.

A few passages in the play will show Moratín's ideas on the subject:

Beatriz (Roque's sister):

> Una niña
> Sin padres, abandonada
> A su tutor, a un bribón,
> Que en lugar de procurarla
> Un casamiento feliz,
> Con un cadáver la casa.
> Act I, scene II

Muñoz, pronouncing his ideas on the marriage, uses a popular phrase, chosen later by Bretón de los Herreros as title for a similar play, "A la vejez viruelas".

And Isabel declares:

> Yo sin tener quien volviera
> Por mí, fuí víctima triste
> De la avaricia perversa
> De mi tutor.
> Act III, scene XIII

Later in the same scene Isabel bewails her fate, to Roque himself and to the audience:

> ¡Ah, señor! ¿Con tantos años
> Aún no tenéis experiencia
> De lo que es una muchacha?
> ¿No sabéis que nos enseñan
> A obedecer ciegamente,
> A que el semblante desmienta
> Lo que sufre el corazón?

Pascual Hernández says that this *comedia* is cold, that its action is languid and hardly dramatic at all.[2] Others, less severe,

---

[2] *Ibid.* page 131.

say that its dramatic merit consists only in the bantering and humorous words of Roque, Muñoz, Beatriz, and Ginés, another servant. These critics are too harsh. *El viejo y la niña* has many moving scenes and the dramatic interest compatible with the severity of the rules of the *comedia clásica*.

The characters in this play are not the original and unforgettable creations of Moratín's master, Molière. Yet certain ones have a striking appeal. Muñoz, the old family retainer, is the most realistic, the most successfully described, the most consistent. He is reminiscent of the *gracioso* of the Siglo de Oro, providing almost all the humor to be found in this serious play. After long service, familiarity between servant and master has grown to such an extent that it is with difficulty that one discerns which is servant and which is master.

Beatriz, Roque's widowed sister, is the next best characterization. She knows Roque well, recognizes the unfortunate character of the marriage Isabel has been forced into, and refuses to leave Roque's home until Isabel can take care of herself.

Roque is not at all attractive, and his marrying Isabel is an unpardonable crime. In the execution of his *comedia* Moratín has portrayed in him a most unflattering representation of the fate that might befall a helpless young girl of the period. But his dependence on Muñoz and the tricks he resorts to to satisfy his suspicions do not give the reader a clear understanding of his character. At the close of the play he laments his actions in a rather melodramatic manner, too easily persuaded of his mistake. Though Roque is the character around whom the play is built, he is the least successfully described and developed, his awakening is too late for remedy, and his conversion is too sudden and unconvincing.

Isabel is a victim of the age. She was imposed upon from the start. But, toward the end of the play she shows some spunk, wakes up to the realization of her plight, and takes the only course open to her, the convent. Without this logical development of her character, realistic and convincing, Isabel might have lost in comparison with the other characters.

El barón was Moratín's second contribution to the Madrid stage. This play, in two acts, in verse, was first presented in the Teatro de la Cruz, January 28, 1803. It deals with the same problem that Moratín used as a basis for his *El viejo y la niña* almost thirteen years before, namely the education of young girls.

The history of the writing and first presentation of *El barón* is unusually interesting. In 1787 Moratín wrote a *zarzuela* called *El barón*. During one of his lengthy absences from Madrid, the play was discovered and altered on several occasions to suit the taste of various groups; it was presented in private homes many times and even in the public theater of Cádiz, though it was hardly recognizable by the time it appeared there. On the return of the author the play was restored to something like its original form. He changed the first act, rewrote the second, and, from a "zarzuela defectuosa compuso una comedia regular".[3]

But Dame Fortune did not smile on the *estreno* of this play. Rivalry between two dramatic troupes, the Ribera and the Caños del Peral, made the opening night noisy, if not successful. The Riberas' *mosqueteros* hissed and applauded shamefully, and, though there were many in the audience who liked the *Barón*, the first performance was a fiasco. But subsequent presentations met with greater approval. It is said even that "el público desapasionado vengó con su aprobación los insultos anteriores, retuvo como frases proverbiales muchas expresiones de la comedia, y desde entonces oye siempre con aprecio esta fábula sencilla, verosímil, cómica, instructiva, y en la cual se observan, como en todas las otras del autor, los preceptos del arte y del buen gusto".[4]

The plot of the play presents few complications. An attractive man, calling himself a baron, comes to stay in the little town of Illescas. He so ingratiates himself with Tía Mónica, a fatuous and ambitious widow, that she invites him to stay in her home, where, through his persuasive manner, he soon assumes the power of master. Blind to his selfish aims, Mónica sees in the "baron" a good match for her daughter Isabel, who is the obedient Moratinian type of heroine. As a result of the suspicions of don Pedro, Mónica's sensible brother, that the baron is an imposter, and through the determination of Leonardo, Isabel's *novio*, the "baron" is exposed as a fraud. He flees just in time to save himself from the *estocada* Leonardo had promised him.

---

[3] *Ibid*, page 131.
[4] *Ibid*, page 131.

Though *El barón* is concerned with essentially the same problem that Moratín treated before, his treatment differs vastly in the two plays. The tone of *El barón* is one of farce, rather than tragedy. Limited by the unity of time (the action of the play lasts from five to ten of one evening), and the simplicity of the action, it is understandable that the author chose to write it in two acts. As a matter of fact, considering the lack of action and the dramatic material, it might have been written in one act. The reader never feels concern as to the outcome of this play, so light is the action and the development of it. Though the setting remains the same throughout (the home of Tía Mónica), there is much going and coming, too many exits and entrances, some of them obviously unnecessary. In this respect Northup's use of the word "juvenilia" is apt description of *El barón*.

With regard to Moratín's presentation of a thesis, his contention is obvious, his ideas appearing early in the first act. And yet, unlike the situation of *El viejo y la niña*, the action is not delayed while someone declaims on the need of more understanding and more freedom of choice for oppressed daughters in the selection of their husbands. But at times, for a line or two, Moratín states most clearly what he did advocate, mentioning even the need for prison reform. This reference seems gratuitous since it has no connection with the plot of the play.

As a vehicle affecting social customs *El barón* may have been effective. We have no way of knowing. It seems quite certain that the play was generally thought to be entertaining. The plot is light, and the purpose of the author is to amuse and to teach while exposing the offending member of society to ridicule. *El barón* is entirely different from *El viejo y la niña* in this respect; one would say that Moratín realized how much more appealing, hence perhaps more effective in reform was this lighter treatment.

The subject of the *mojigata* has long been popular with Spanish authors. Harking back to *Marta la piadosa*, if not earlier, *La mojigata* is Moratín's contribution to the collection of hypocrite plays. In three acts, in verse, it was first presented in the Teatro de la Cruz, May 19, 1804.

Adhering closely to his advocacy of a broader education of young girls, Moratín takes as an example a case in which a father is the culpable parent rather than the mother, as in *El barón*, or a false tutor in *El viejo y la niña*.

Clara, the *mojigata*, has been too strictly reared for her own good, and as a result of her harsh, unbending father's insistence on perfection, she, pretending always to be pious, has succeeded in making him believe her perfect. Though she is continually telling her father how eager she is to enter a convent, she is not so unworldly as he thinks. Other people know her better, though she is not guilty of any grave wrongdoing. Her cousin Inés is betrothed to Claudio, an eccentric young man. And neither of the girls is happy with her prospect for the future. Inés is a normal, well-educated young lady, while Claudio and Clara are unusual personalities. Claudio, however, has become enamored of Clara, and asks his servant, Perico, to assist him in his suit. This proves easy, because she wants to marry and to leave the oppressive custody of her father.

The play is long and too complex for such an apparently simple situation. The reason for this unusual length is that the father's reactionary ideas on education must be set forth. Luis, his brother, and Inés must be shown to be a normal, sensible father-daughter team, in contrast with the other father and daughter. Perico, evidently played by a popular actor of the time, had to have his lines.

Outwardly, then, *La mojigata* is a typical Moratinian play, written to amuse and to teach. As we see from the notes to the available edition, Moratín was required to make a few changes in the original manuscript before the play could be presented. The subject of the *mojigata*, though quite familiar to the Spaniard, is a delicate matter with the Catholic church. Moratín was dealing with a theme which the ecclesiastical censor was sure to find distasteful. And such was the case when the censor read it. Five lengthy passages were expurgated before it could be presented. Each of them shows in some way Clara's superficial character or is an unflattering comparison of a nun's life with that of a happily married woman.

Padding seems to be a failing with Moratín. The actors and actresses of the Cruz company had to be cared for, of course. Tío Juan, a demandadero, Lucía, a servant, and Perico (Claudio's servant), are minor figures. These characters, however, add little to the play's essential theme or action. The plot is intentionally complicated by and for them. Mainly due to the actics of Perico, there are some entertaining comic scenes, and these may seem to justify the play's unusual length.

It is impossible to read this play without remembering Molière and especially his *Tartuffe*. Yet, though the two plays have a similar subject —hypocrisy— the two treatments are vastly different. Clara is in no way the unforgettable Tartuffe. Larra says in his short critique of the *comedia* that *La mojigata* can never be compared with Tartuffe, but, he hastens to add, Moratín's dénouement is "infinitamente superior" to that of Molière's play. Larra goes on to say that the principal merit of *La mojigata* is in Moratín's accurate and interesting depiction of local customs, its humor, its delicate satire, and in his effective manner of presenting ideas. Larra concludes with what we regard as self-evident, that Molière is more universal than Moratín; the latter is more local, more restrictive, his fame consequently less enduring.[5]

Perico, a minor character, enjoys the most attention, speaks the best lines, having many of the qualities, attributes, and failings of the *gracioso* of the Golden Age. His part is enhanced by his appearing in a grotesque disguise in order to appropriate a large sum of money, destined originally for a convent, but now to be used to pay the pawnbroker and his master's (Claudio's) debts. Perico is an interesting character, but he occupies the stage too much of the time for one who was intended to be a minor figure.

Clara is convincing as the "piadosa", a clever characterization. At the slightest suggestion or stimulus, she begins to preach, while everyone, but her father, knows her to be a hypocrite, though we are never led to regard her as wicked.

Claudio is odd, eccentric. Just why Moratín describes him so is difficult to understand. He may be characterized, aside from the slapstick possibilities the part affords, as a fitting punishment for Clara. He is rather uninteresting, a loose characterization, in spite of the attention given him.

The two brothers, Martín and Luis, like the cousins Clara and Inés, are portrayed as the personifications of contrasting ideas

---

[5] *Ibid*, page 212.

on education, each of their daughters representing the result of opposing types. Martín's failings seem to be overemphasized, and onstage this would assume greater significance than it seems to have when read only.

Having acquired experience by writing what are considered his three lesser works, Moratín wrote the play for which he is best known, *El sí de las niñas,* in three acts and in prose, first presented in the Teatro de la Cruz in Madrid, January 24, 1806. In *El sí de las niñas* Moratín tries to show how wrong it is for parents to insist on absolute control of their daughters, allowing no freedom of self-expression in the choice of a husband.

In order to present his thesis, Moratín had to imagine extremely unusual conditions. Diego, a man of fifty-nine, wants a wife who has been carefully guarded from the temptations of the world. To meet these requirements the author created Francisca, a girl of sixteen, who has lived in a convent since the age of twelve. Unknown to Diego or Irene, Francisca's egocentric mother, Francisca left the convent on one occasion, when she met Diego's nephew, who has assumed the name of Félix, lest Diego learn he has been absent from duty in the army. After the first interview Carlos has met Francisca secretly at a window of the convent every night for three months, though it is difficult to understand how their means of identification (three handclaps, to be answered by three more) was not enough to betray their meetings. When Diego learns that Francisca is not innocent of worldly knowledge, and when he realizes how unfair it would be to marry her against her wishes, he is persuaded to relinquish his claims upon her. It is not too difficult after all for him to accept her as a daughter.

We are told that *El sí de las niñas* is at least in part based on an unfortunate experience of the author's in which he himself loved a younger girl, and this affection was not reciprocated. If we accept the idea of the secret meetings of Francisca and Carlos not being discovered, the other incidents are plausible, but Moratín has to distort the plot somewhat to present his lesson. It seems strange that a very young girl (16) should go traipsing about unnoticed by any of her guardians. And stranger still that Carlos, a high-ranking officer of the army should risk dishonor, a court martial, and even a sentence of death by going AWOL. Then too at the end of the play it seems that Diego is rather easily persuaded not to pursue his ill-considered matrimonial designs.

As for the characterization, whereas Moratín has created two excellent characters in Diego and Irene, the characters of Carlos and Francisca are unrealistic and suffer by comparison. Francisca and Carlos are so completely subservient to their mother and guardian respectively that Francisca is but a child, and Carlos is treated as a schoolboy, though he is supposed to be a heroic colonel in the army of Spain.

It is of interest to note that *El sí de las niñas* and Rojas's *Entre bobos anda el juego* are much alike both in plot and in characters. In the latter play the *figurón* Lucas sends his nephew Pedro for his (Lucas's) betrothed, Isabel de Peralta. Her father, Antonio, like Francisca's mother, Irene, is much concerned with his own financial future, which is to be assured by the coming marriage of his daughter and Lucas, who has a great deal of money. However, Pedro, like Carlos, has met the lady before, and has fallen in love with her. Like *El sí de las niñas* in that the events take place at an inn, Lucas finds Pedro in Isabel's room, and suspecting the worst, has them married, promising at the same time no financial assistance. Even the minor characters of *El sí de las niñas* are strongly reminiscent of those of *Entre bobos anda el juego* in number, purpose, and actions.

In *Entre bobos anda el juego* Lucas is treated with ridicule to impress the audience with the impropriety in an older man's marrying a young girl. Moratín, however, does not take this point of view. As José Mariano de Larra says in a criticism of a presentation of the play in 1834, Moratín has real sympathy with the problem and treats it with understanding. An atmosphere of melancholy, not farce, pervades the whole play, though the servants enliven some scenes with typical small talk. Moratín was the first comic author in Spain to give "a lachrymose and sentimental character" to a play of this type, a genre in which his predecessors had only held the elderly man to ridicule.[6] We never feel any antipathy toward Diego, because he is attractively presented throughout. When at last he realizes the unfairness

---

[6] LARRA, JOSÉ MARIANO DE: "Representación de *El sí de las niñas*" in "La Revista Española", 1834, pages 131-133; *Clásicos castellanos*, vol. 58, Madrid, 1924.

of Irene's wishes and his own desires, he is shown to be self-effacing and kindly toward his nephew and his betrothed, generously stepping aside in favor of Carlos.

The two characters, Diego and Irene, are really exceptional. They are real people, cleverly played against one another, though at first they are working toward the same goal. Carlos, however, is not the ardent lover one would expect to see. The characterization of Francisca is hard to accept, even though she is but sixteen. She is too submissive to be real. On the other hand, the contrast in character between Diego, just, generous, and logical, and Irene, selfish and ignorant, is perfect.

Moratín is notably successful in suggesting the need of reform, though he might have presented his views on the subject with more subtlety. When Diego pronounces his views (the author's), as he does several times, the action of the play is stopped completely

Apparently, in Spain early in the nineteenth century, young girls were sometimes compelled to marry men old enough to be their grandfathers. The author observes that there is serious need for reform with regard to this custom, but he does not give a remedy. He sees the wrong, but proposes no emancipation of women, which would have been the real solution. He prefers to attack the way young girls were trained, blaming the situation on the selfish personal consideration of their parents.

Carlos casts aside his usually ineffectual manner toward the end of the play to remind Diego that, though the latter may soon be officially married to Francisca, who would remain faithful to him, she would never love him, and that her first love and only love would always be his, Carlos's. This seems part of the moral lesson.

At the end of the last act Diego points up the moral lesson when he calls attention to the young couple's good fortune in learning the truth of the situation and preventing what would have been a grave mistake. He adds, "¡Ay de aquellos que lo saben tarde!". These pronouncements are not examples of good dramatic technique, yet they fit into the normal course of don Diego's thinking and experience. The lesson would have been as readily acceptable, if Moratín had merely illustrated his point of view, leaving the conclusion to the audience.

Although *El sí de las niñas* enjoyed unusual prosperity (it was presented twenty-six days in January and February, 1806, at the Cruz Theater, closing only because of the coming of the Lenten season), its timeliness could not endure. The play is "dated", its timeliness no more, but it is still a good play because of its characters.

As Larra pointed out, when he wrote a criticism of a performance of this play in 1834, this manner of teaching a lesson is an essential difference between Moratín and Molière. The latter addresses his play to the intellect and persuades by presenting the laughable side of things. Moratín relates the ridiculous aspects of a situation, but he appeals to the heart by presenting at the same time the results of the *extravío*, in this case the proposed alliance. With reference to the frequent comparison between Moratín and Molière, the inscription on the Silvela pantheon in Paris, where Moratín was first buried, calls him "the Spanish Molière".

Later in the nineteenth century another playwright and critic, Ventura de la Vega, came to the defence of *El sí de las niñas*. At the Teatro de la Cruz in 1848 this writer presented his one-act play in prose, "La crítica de *El sí de las niñas*". In the entertaining little critique we find characters with the same names and traits of those of *El sí de las niñas* and *El café*, another well-known play by Moratín. These characters come and go during and after the supposed performance of *El sí de las niñas* and comment on the work. All but one of them criticize Moratín's play in the same terms that it had been criticized before: that the important personages of all Moratín's good plays —*El barón, La mojigata, El café*, and *El sí de las niñas*— are alike; that all four plays are plagiarisms of Molière; that it is only a "disertación en diálogo, que quieren llamar drama"; and, that Francisca and Carlos certainly do not act like normal lovers. To offset this unfavorable judgment, the poet and critic in *La crítica* defends *El sí de las niñas*, declaring that even in 1848, some forty years after the first presentation, *El sí de las niñas* was called "la joya del teatro moderno". Ventura de la Vega goes on to say that, though the invasion of the Romantic genre had almost banished *El sí de las niñas* from the stage, in 1848 it had reappeared in the repertory and was eagerly received. Ventura de la Vega thus defends

Moratín's masterpiece, calling it the drama nearest perfection that he knew. Though times have changed, he maintains that it is still a good play. [7]

Reviewing the four plays by Moratín discussed here, we are impressed at once by their similarity in a central theme. In each of them the author endeavors to present his ideas on education for young girls, reflecting on the Spanish customs of the late eighteenth and early nineteenth centuries. Each play advances the plea for greater liberty in education, more freedom of self-expression, an appeal for honesty on the part of those entrusted with their care and training. Moratín's drama is essentially of the thesis type, in that he proposes to change for the better the antiquated, unfair, unrealistic practices prevalent at the time in regard to the education of young girls. He urges that the girls be allowed to develop their natural likes and dislikes, with guidance, but without the absolute authority of ambitious domineering parents and tutors.

Though this is the purpose of all four of these *comedias*, the problem —essentially the same— is treated differently, and with increasing success with each play. In *El viejo y la niña* the young girl has already been married to the *setentón*. This, then, is a more serious play than the next three, and is indeed a tragedy. But in *El barón, La mojigata,* and *El sí de las niñas,* a happy ending is easily and logically arranged. In *El barón* and *La mojigata* we find many elements of the farce.

As is usually the case when a playwright has a thesis to present, the dramatic values of the work suffer. In some scenes, notably in *El sí de las niñas*, the action of the play stops altogether while the *raisonneur* (don Diego, here) preaches the sermon, and presents in no uncertain terms the author's views on the subject. Nevertheless, in the majority of the scenes the purpose is masterfully built into the play—it is evident, but usually unobtrusive.

Moratín's originality in character creation is his most outstanding feature. All of his leading characters have something of the eccentric about them: Irene in *El sí de las niñas* is unforgettable as the scheming, imperious *materfamilias*, while Diego recalls the

---

[7] VENTURA DE LA VEGA, *Obras completas*, Barcelona, 1894.

figurón at its best. Moratín's characterizations show his interest in and accurate knowledge of the bourgeoisie, and each of the plays deals with this social class. There is not the combination of nobility and bourgeois to be found in the works of Beaumarchais, for example, nor had Spanish drama reached the concern for the proletariat it showed later in the works of Dicenta. But the ideas for change are on the march, and it is to Moratín that the credit is due for initiating this form of drama on the modern Spanish stage.

The greatest literary critic of the nineteenth century had this to say about *El sí de las niñas* in his article "Representación de la comedia nueva de don Manuel Gorostiza, titulada *Contigo pan y cebolla*", in a discussion of *locas bodas y desatinados enlaces*. Larra says: "Los autores dramáticos van, sin embargo, con los tiempos; la recogida educación de los jóvenes del siglo pasado autorizaba la tiranía de los padres, y Moratín creyó hacer un señalado servicio a su país dando *El sí de las niñas*. De entonces acá hemos andado con pasos agigantados; y las costumbres del día, más que de la tiranía de los padres, resiéntense de la licencia e insubordinación de los hijos. Esto no es debido tampoco únicamente a las novelas. Otros muchos libros ha sido preciso escribir, muchas revoluciones de todas especies han debido pasar por los pueblos; otros hombres, a más de los novelistas, habían tenido que nacer antes para dar este impulso extraordinario en poco más de medio siglo al entendimiento humano. El hecho es con todo positivo; el abuso existe y reclama urgentemente la férula del poeta cómico. En el siglo actual se pueden contar tantas desgraciadas víctimas de los enlaces poco meditados, como en el pasado de las obligadas reclusiones de entonces." [8]

It is clear, then, that Larra appreciated the value of Moratín's dramatic efforts as instruments of social influence and importance, even as late as 1833, some twenty-seven years after the first presentation of *El sí de las niñas*. Indeed, Moratín's influence was to appear in much of the dramatic literature of nineteenth-century Spain.

---

[8] LARRA, "Representación de la comedia nueva de don Eduardo Gorostiza, titulada *Contigo pan y cebolla*". *Colección de los mejores autores españoles*, vol. XLVII.

CHAPTER II

CONTINUATORS OF THE MORATÍN TRADITION

Fourteen years were to pass before Martínez de la Rosa (1787-1862), brought to the Spanish stage anything comparable to the successful dramatic works of Moratín. In the tragic period of the reign of Fernando VII the comedies of Martínez de la Rosa must have been welcome relief from the troubled state of affairs which prevailed in Spain from the invasion of the French armies in 1808 to the end of the tyrant Fernando's unhappy misrule in 1833. In addition to the moving tragedies, *La conjuración de Venecia* and *Aben Humeya*, the man who was one day (1834) to become prime minister wrote several entertaining comedies. The first of these to appear was a two-act comedy in prose, *Lo que puede un empleo,* presented in Cádiz in 1812.

The plot is simple. As a result of the influence of Melitón, a self-righteous, hypocritical, reactionary, tale-bearing "friend", Fabián forbids his daughter Carlota ever to see her fiance Teodoro again. Melitón has denounced him as a "liberal". Before matters become too critical, however, Luis, Teodoro's father, with a clever ruse, exposes Melitón as the self-seeking hypocrite that he is. Fabián admits his own blindness, acknowledges his error in judgment, and grants Teodoro and Carlota permission to marry.

It might be advisable to insert a word of explanation here. The term, "liberal" had at the time this play was written an extremely unsavory significance. Upon the return from exile of "el deseado", "el rey absoluto", as the unenlightened populace called Fernando VII, the liberal Cortes, formed in Madrid and Cádiz, for example, with the purpose of establishing a republic, or at least a more democratic form of government, were dissolved; and "liberal" acquired in some quarters the connotation of traitor. Hence Melitón's use of the word would be comparable to the term of opprobium, frequently and carelessly used today: communist.

In the *advertencia* in the available edition of this play, the author states his purpose: "El vivo deseo de presentar en el teatro a cierta clase de hipócritas-políticos, que so color de religión se oponen entre nosotros a las benéficas reformas me estimuló a emprender, como un mero pasatiempo, la composición de esta comedia. Primer ensayo mío en tan difícil ramo, proyectada y concluida en el corto espacio de una semana y sin haber recibido ni corrección ni lima, no puedo lisonjearme de que tenga ningún mérito literario; pero habiendo merecido en el teatro unos aplausos, muy superiores a los que jamás pude prometerme, y habiendo hecho reir a costa de los que, por ignorancia o por malicia, intentan desacreditar las nuevas instituciones, me he decidido a imprimirla, deseando contribuir de todos modos a que el público conozca a los enemigos de nuestra libertad". [1]

The author's purpose is clear: to call attention to the immoral conditions of the era in which he lived. He has succeeded in portraying an all too prevalent vice, that a person will do anything for a job or sinecure. He will renounce all principles, refuse to accept anything new solely on the grounds that it is new, and even intentionally destroy the happiness of others. All of these undesirable traits are to be found in the character of Melitón. As Melitón is a priest, his failing is designed to call attention to hypocrisy among the clergy. Though a few humorous lines relieve the monotony of the "sermons" which the play contains, there is little to recommend the play. The Moratinian influence is apparent, but in Moratín's works there is the redeeming feature of the creation of some good characters, realistic, interesting, almost flesh and blood creations: those in *Lo que puede un empleo* do not attain that degree of eminence.

Martínez de la Rosa was very nearly correct in his modest declaration that "este primer ensayo no tenga ningún mérito literario". The playwright, something of the opportunist, was taking

---

[1] Obras dramáticas de don F. Martínez de la Rosa, Vol. I, Madrid, 1861, page V.

advantage of the times, appealing to the memories the Spanish people had of the events of a few months before, when, with the formation of the Junta, the appearance of the Constitution, and the expulsion of the French invaders, they may have had the fond hope of obtaining the previously unheard of privilege of the freedom of the press mentioned in this *comedia*.

The second play by Martínez de la Rosa was *La niña en casa y la madre en máscara*. This *comedia* in three acts, in verse, was first presented in Madrid in 1821. In the *advertencia* accompanying this rather long play (the third act is as long as the first and second combined), Martínez de la Rosa said: "Como el mejor de nuestros poetas cómicos modernos había ya presentado en varios cuadros las resultas de la educación apocada y monjil, que solía darse a las hijas en España, me propuse por argumento de esta composición censurar un vicio diferente, más común en el estado actual de nuestras costumbres, cual es el que origina, en el teatro del mundo, del mal ejemplo y del descuido de las madres". He goes on to say by way of recommendation, "El público, al parecer, ha juzgado fiel la pintura: habiendo acogido favorablemente esta comedia, representada por primera vez en Madrid, a fines del año de 1821, y posteriormente en los demás de teatros de España, y en algunos de América." Of interest too is the information that a vaudeville in two acts, *La mère au bal et la fille à la maison*, with the same theme and principal situations, and written by Martínez de la Rosa, was presented "con gran éxito" in Paris.

In *La niña en casa y la madre en máscara* Leoncia is the *madre en máscara* who keeps her daughter Inés too much *en casa*, while she, the mother, is always on the go at *tertulias, bailes,* and *máscaras*. The daughter seems to have become enamored of Teodoro, a friend of her mother's; and, when he, pretending to love her, asks her to marry him, she accepts. When he asks Leoncia, rather surprisingly to her, for her permission to marry her daughter, she is so astonished at the thought that her daughter can have such ideas, that she orders Teodoro from the house. A sly character (recalling the "barón" in Moratín's play by the same name), Teodoro knew that Inés was in the wings, so to speak, overhearing the conversation. Later Teodoro tells Leoncia that he was only pretending to request permission to marry Inés for Inés's benefit, saying that "como niña" she thought she was in love with him.

He declares, however, that he is really in love with her (Leoncia). He goes on to say that his actions had been governed by a desire to remove suspicion from her (Leoncia), since he knew that they were being watched. Convinced by Teodoro that there is nothing between him and Inés, Leoncia goes to the ball she planned to attend, returning home late, to find that Teodoro has persuaded Inés to run away with him. Fortunately he had been surprised in the act of eloping by Leoncia's brother and Inés's sincere suitor, Luis. Leoncia recognizes her mistakes, promises to be a good mother, and addresses Luis as "hijo".

La niña en casa y la madre en máscara is essentially a serious *comedia*, relieved only occasionally by the humorous sallies of the servants Perico and Juana.

As is usually the case with a play of this type, the action frequently is stopped or is at best only delayed, by excessive preaching and moralizing. One speech of Luis seems to echo the ideas of Diego in *El sí de las niñas:*

> "¿Desde los años más tiernos
> A qué enseñan a las niñas?
> A ocultar dentro del pecho
> Los gustos más inocentes,
> A disfrazar sus deseos,
> A desmentir con sus voces."

So, when Inés confesses her desires, begging her mother's permission to marry Teodoro (though this would have been a mistake, and we are led to believe that Inés would have recognized Teodoro for what he was if she had received the proper education), Leoncia cannot believe these are really her daughter's ideas. Indeed, she hardly knows her daughter, she is away so much of the time.

Yet in *La niña en casa y la madre en máscara* we find a happy combination of preaching and of entertainment. The tone is usually serious, but not monotonous. The purpose of the author is clear, and his thesis is rather painlessly assimilated. We do not find the moral unpleasant or distastefully presented. The social problem is skillfully associated with the author's dramatic problem, namely, to let Luis win Inés. This is reasonably enough introduced in the opening scene. And Luis is presented in such a way that we want him to attain his goal.

The custom of observing the unities is maintained here with apparent ease. Though the time elapsing from beginning to end is not declared, so much has happened beforehand and the action seems to begin at such a critical point, that the succeeding events, though many, could plausibly occur in the course of one day with no technical difficulty or strain on the imagination. All in all, *La niña en casa y la madre en máscara* is a generally entertaining play. As Valbuena-Prat says, "Es la mejor producción de estilo moratiniano que merece ponerse al lado de las obras secundarias del modelo; tiene una cierta gracia ágil y "beaumarchaisca' lo que hace agradable aunque un poco tímido el resultado".

La boda y el duelo was the next *comedia moratiniana* written by Martínez de la Rosa, a *comedia* in three acts, in verse, first presented in 1820. The scene is a room in the home of the Marquesa del Roble. Luisa, a girl of twenty years of age, is betrothed by her ambitious mother, the Marquesa del Roble, to don Juan, a retired brigadier general, old enough to be Luisa's grandfather. Luisa's real love is Carlos, who returns from the university of Salamanca on the day of the wedding. In his anger and jealousy he challenges Juan to a duel, which serves only to make the good-hearted Juan recognize the fact that Luisa and Carlos love each other and that he would be doing Luisa a grave injustice in marrying her against her will.

The most striking thing about this *comedia* is its similarity to Moratín's *El sí de las niñas*. In fact, it is almost an echo of the earlier play in plot, characters, and situations, which are nearly identical. Kindhearted don Diego is like don Juan; the financially embarrassed *marquesa* is Irene over again; the obedient Francisca becomes the docile Luisa; and Carlos remains Carlos, but in name only. The same kind of moralizing by the same kind of characters is present. The shock expressed by the *marquesa* on learning of her daughter's love for Carlos is the exact representation of her counterpart's reaction in *El sí de las niñas*. The general, like Diego, finds out that his betrothed is being forced into the marriage by a not too unselfish or too self-effacing mother; all the major characters except Carlos are the mirrored counterparts of those of *El sí de las niñas*. Carlos, on the other hand, is an improvement on his *tocayo*. The new Carlos is the fiery, headstrong, quick-tempered lover one might expect him to be, even challenging the old soldier to a duel. In this, then, Martínez de la Rosa succeeds where Moratín fails, but the other characters, though good imitations, are not the equal of Moratín's characterizations.

But *La boda y el duelo*, like most sequels, is not as good as its predecessor. Intentionally humorous scenes are not nearly so funny as the priceless ones with Calamocha, Simón, and the other servants, reminiscent of the best of the Golden Age. And the weakest point in this dramatic creation is the superabundance of characters. They are introduced almost at random: Joaquín, Juan's nephew; a *condesa*, serving some use as a *confidente* for Luisa; Juana, Luisa's duenna; a *demandero*, calling for a scene which contributes little to subsequent action; a host of musicians who do not play long enough to make their presence worthwhile; a swarm of lackeys who add but little; and last, and least important at the close of the last act, Teresa, another new character, is introduced!—violating a cardinal principle of good dramatic technique. She says a few inconsequential words, then faints; this occasions a little dialect from the lackeys, and in the pronunciation of the words they speak there is some humor, but the situation is not exceptionally funny. In the last act the greatest criticism must be made of the padding. Martínez de la Rosa's plot just did not have enough action to fill out this act, so he resorted to the insertion of extra characters and extra scenes designed to amuse, but advancing the essential action not a whit.

As Martínez de la Rosa declared in the *advertencia* accompanying *La boda y el duelo*, he was trying to write a "comedia de la escuela de Moratín". It is certainly that, but is hardly more than an inferior imitation; however, it is generally entertaining in that it is an echo of Moratín's popular play. And this in itself reveals Martínez's principal weakness in the type of play under consideration, his lack of originality. There are but few really dramatic situations, usually seeming forced, and failing to be resultant from or introductory to other situations naturally and easily. The tone is not really serious in spite of the tears in the opening scenes. Carlos's return and his letter to don Juan are the keys to most of the dramatic action, and both of these are developed fairly well.

Of the Moratinian plays of Martínez de la Rosa, Menéndez y Pelayo says: "Son la dramatización de un aforismo de moral doméstica. Todo está en su lugar, nada desentona; todo arguye talento; se respira bien; se vive entre gentes de buena crianza; ...sólo una cosa está ausente desde el principio al fin, la poesía, así de dicción, como de sentimiento".

Hurtado y González Palencia in their *Historia de la Literatura Española* say: "Todas son comedias de corte moratiniano, de gran sencillez en la acción, de escaso movimiento en los incidentes, de estilo cuidado, de tendencia moralizadora y de pocos rasgos verdaderamente chistosos". Of all three of these *comedias* the same observation might be made: not very sophisticated comedy, little action in a plot set among people of the middle class, consciously imitative of Moratín, and rarely poetic.

In conclusion, we can see clearly the Moratinian influence in the works of Martínez de la Rosa. Both men felt deeply about the vices they satirized in these seven plays. They intended to entertain as they criticized, and in most cases they were reasonably successful. It is significant to note here that the vice criticized is similar in each of these plays: the education of young girls and the hypocrisy which is induced and encouraged by faulty education practices. Though there is enough variety of presentation and treatment of this theme of a broader education for women, the idea of emancipation of women is never a part of the program of either playwright. Absolute authority over the lives of their daughters was rather the prerogative of the parents. This is what Moratín and Martínez de la Rosa attacked, showing in each play the tragic results to be expected of the narrow, confining, hypocritical upbringing usually imposed on young girls of the period.

As we read the plays by Moratín, we note that the Molière influence on Moratín appears almost as often as the latter's influence on Martínez de la Rosa. But neither of the pupils attained the success of his tutor-mentor. Molière's universality still appeals. The *comedias* of Moratín and of Martínez de la Rosa are dated, not at all suitable for presentation today, interesting only as a reflection of the customs of the period.

About the time Martínez de la Rosa was writing for the stage, another playwright was presenting some lighter *comedias* with similar success. Manuel Gorostiza (1789-1851), a Mexican who spent most of his life in Spain, wrote several *comedias* with a thesis element which followed the Moratín tradition. Gorostiza's theme in *Indulgencia para todos*, 1818, is in a sense an enlargement of Moratín's purpose in that Gorostiza satirizes intolerance, which is not an exclusively Spanish failing, but is, rather, universal.

The manner in which Gorostiza presents his ideas on the subject of intolerance is novel and interesting. Severo, the man selected by Fermín to be the *novio* of his daughter Tomasa, is a person of rare gifts, possessing all the qualities that Fermín believes essential in a son-in-law—elegance, breeding, and *savoir faire*. His son Carlos, however, though a close friend of Severo's reminds Fermín that Severo, with all his apparent perfection, is extremely intolerant of failings in others. In order to find out if this is true, to test Severo's humanness, they contrive to expose him to several carefully prepared and difficult situations. Carlos tells Severo that Tomasa is his (Carlos's) *novia*, later arranges to have them be surprised alone, which leads Carlos to challenge Severo to a duel. They play other tricks on him, which he, surprisingly enough, meets calmly and in a competent, determined manner, indicating also that he has other more important attributes, in addition to possessing the superficial qualities which Fermín esteemed so highly. Thus he is revealed as a suitable *yerno*.

Indulgencia para todos, while advocating tolerance, is also, like other plays already mentioned, a mild form of satire on education. In the play Fermín inadvertently admits his strictness in rearing Tomasa, confidently declaring that she will offer no resistance to his plan to marry her to Severo, because she is "sin voluntad propia",—surely an echo of Moratín. We are not, however, presented with a lengthy oration near the end of the play, nor are we reminded of the need of broader education for young girls: the lesson is apparent through the natural development of the plot. At the beginning of the play Fermín is the blind, unthinking, selfish father, but like most of Moratín's offenders, Fermín is an apt pupil, and while teaching Severo his lesson (with the help of his son Carlos), Fermín learns his lesson of tolerance too.

The moralizing delivered almost *ad infinitum* in the earlier thesis plays is reduced to a desirable degree in this play by Gorostiza. Of course, the whole play is a moral lesson urging tolerance, but at times, indeed during most of the play, the plot is sufficient to engross the audience. Aside from some overlong speeches, which add little to the actual development of the play, this is a very humorous piece, yet clearly *de tendencia moralizadora*. Carlos, in the skillful way he lies to Severo while playing a trick on him, recalls that delightful scene in *La verdad sospechosa* in which García lies so handily to his father to the dismay of the younger man's counselor.

Except for the artificial stratagem executed by and at the direction of Carlos and Fermín, the plot is simple and cleverly developed. The "play within a play" idea is successfully handled. The characters are realistic and plausible. Gorostiza observes the unities too. *Indulgencia para todos* is indeed what Hurtado y González Palencia say Gorostiza's plays were—a "galería de costumbres".

Still another play which contains a "thesis element" is *Las costumbres de antaño o la pesadilla,* a one-act piece. In it don Pedro is such a devotee of the "remembrance of things past", so unreasonably conscious of customs and events of the *Edad Media,* that he has made life for his niece and nephew who live with him almost unbearable. As Félix the nephew says:

> ... ... al cabo
> todo el mundo es esclavo
> del capricho de mi tío;
> y si aquesto no influyera
> en su genio y condición,
> pudiéramos con razón
> pasarle tanta quimera;
> mas, por la Virgen, señor,
> si no se puede sufrir.

Everything they do seems wrong to him. So, they (Félix and Isabel, the niece) and the latter's *novio*, determine to play a trick on him to try to bring him to his senses. Don Pedro, awakening one day from a long *siesta* is met by someone who calls himself his *escudero*, who leads him into believing that he has been transported to the fifteenth century. As might be expected, he finds life not so attractive as he had imagined it, customs too rigorous, and long-accustomed comforts lacking. Just before being forced to participate in a tournament, knowing nothing of jousting, Pedro, terrified, wakes up, and rejoicing to be again in the nineteenth century, admits his error, granting Isabel and her *novio* permission to marry.

Especially interesting as representative of Gorostiza's "galería de costumbres", *Las costumbres de antaño* is also a slightly satirical jesting at excessive devotion to antiquated customs, in the nineteenth century a provocative subject dear to the most progressive of Spain's writers.

Every scene is packed with humor. The tone is gay and amusing throughout. Don Pedro would have to be played by a successful comic actor if the author's work were to have the maximum success. The little play intending to depict the transition between the centuries one would have to accept as one accepts it in the "Connecticut Yankee", but this scene could be presented realistically. It is an entertaining little play.

Last of the plays by Gorostiza under consideration is *Don Dieguito*, first presented in 1820. Not only does the title recall Moreto's play *El lindo don Diego,* but the delineation of the main character certainly indicates familiarity with the Golden Age *comedia*. Of course, *El lindo don Diego* was modelled upon Guillén de Castro's *El Narciso en su opinión*, and this too may have been borrowed from some predecessor. At any rate, *Don Dieguito* is more of a *comedia de figurón* than any of those studied so far, continuing also the tradition of Moratín, and through him Molière.

In this five-act play in verse Gorostiza seems to be trying to satirize, ridicule, and jest at many things. In all but one of the principal characters there is some failing in need of correction: petimetry (French: *petit maitre*), positivism, ambition, adulation, and—again—education of young girls. Opposed to all these is one sensible real character who successfully teaches each of the culprits a useful lesson.

The plot is simple and even obvious. Anselmo, a rich man from Santander, arrives unexpectedly in Madrid to see his nephew Diego, whom he discovers to be a fop, a dandy, nothing like the man he was before coming to Madrid. He is living in the home of Cleto, who, together with his wife María, is trying to arrange a marriage with their daughter Adelaida, only to get the inheritance of Diego, whom they suppose to be a very rich man. Anselmo is quick to size up the situation and tells the family that he is going to get married. This is bad news, because it means that Diego will not inherit the money which they covet so much. So, Adelaida opportunely transfers her affection to Anselmo. He in turn advises them either to arrange the marriage of Diego and Adelaida or tell Diego to leave their home. At this point all three insult Diego so intensely that, fatuous though he is, he understands, and Anselmo has saved his nephew from the trap. Having done so, he announces that he has lost all his money, and, taking Diego with him, he leaves for Santander and home.

Many hilarious scenes accompany this generally interesting plot. The dialogue is especially effective, facile, and versatile, as good dialogue is one of Gorostiza's outstanding characteristics as a playwright. The mood is always gay, optimistic, and amusing. As for character-portrayal, Gorostiza is consistent and successful. Yet none of these creations is original or outstanding. Dieguito is the dandy, concerned with his versifying attempts, doggerel which he delights in reading to anyone, expecting, of course, praise which he does not deserve. He thrives on flattery, as does Cleto, his prospective *suegro*. But it is clearly indicated that he is loved only for his money, and he is purposely left in a ridiculous position at the conclusion to the play, though this seems, as stated before, a fortunate escape for Dieguito. The type of *figurón* that Dieguito represents is ridiculed mercilessly, and worst of all by the girl whom he expected to marry. Certainly Gorostiza's characterization of Dieguito is unflattering in the extreme. Anselmo, Diego's uncle, is the only reasonable person in the play. He effectively arranges Dieguito's escape and the disappointment of his would-be featherbedding in-laws. Not clever or especially charming, in fact usually brusque, Anselmo is the natural contrast to this group, which seems to represent Madrid society.

Though *Don Dieguito* is a piece intended to ridicule certain failings, practices, and foibles, in its satire it could not draw disapproval from any quarter. The tone, the aims, and the victims are all too generalized, too innocuous for that.

It is obvious that Gorostiza's treatment is different from Moratín's, especially in the tone, characters, and purpose. In short, *Don Dieguito,* like the other plays by Gorostiza discussed here, seems a comedy of manners, not essentially a thesis play. The moral lesson, and a lesson is to be derived from any dramatic work, after all, is readily recognized and assimilated through the skillful creation of entertaining scenes, for the characters do not take time out from the action of the play to preach openly against dandyism or the other social weaknesses Gorostiza felt called upon to criticize.

One of the most prolific dramatists (110 original plays) of the nineteenth century was Bretón de los Herreros. Like his contemporary Gorostiza, he continued the tradition of Moratín with many amusing comedies, one of which is included here as exemplary of those works which, if not primarily thesis drama, at least contain a "thesis element".

Such a play is *A Madrid me vuelvo,* a three-act *comedia* in verse presented in the Teatro del Príncipe, January 25, 1828. The scene is a village in the Sierra de Cameros, in the home of Baltasar, in the year 1828.

Ambitious Baltasar is about to marry his obedient daughter Carmen to Esteban, the wealthy son of Matea. Bernardo, Baltasar's brother, satiated with his aimless life at the court, leaves Madrid to seek peace and quiet in the little *pueblo* where Baltasar lives. Learning of his tyrant brother's plans, fair-minded Bernardo determines to arrange matters so that Carmen may marry Felipe, the *novio* of her choice. Here, the grotesquely comic Matea appears, forbidding Esteban to marry Carmen, who Matea thinks is not worthy of her son. He, though much older than Carmen, is still completely subservient to his mother, and the marriage is mutually cancelled, permitting Felipe and Carmen to marry. And Bernardo, astonished at the unexpected character of small-town life, declares that he is returning to Madrid.

Though the main purpose of this play is to amuse, Bretón de los Herreros has included enough of the thesis element to qualify it as a thesis play. The lesson is that of *El sí de las niñas*, namely, against the strict education of young girls and the intrusive interest on the part of parents in the selection of husbands for them. Bretón presents his thesis in a much more direct manner than Moratín had done, for he has drawn Baltasar so demanding, so insistent on having his way, at times so violent, that he out-Irenes Irene. In spite of this, however, our interest is not drawn especially to the plight of the girl Carmen, which Moratín had so deftly succeeded in doing with Isabel in *El sí de las niñas*. Rather, we are presented with a group of unusual characters who make amusing speeches, but frequently the action is so crowded with comic elements that the lesson is of minor importance. In fact, the lesson is presented only by the shockingly arbitrary manner in which Bretón forces the dénouement. No crisis ever occurs, for Baltasar, after ranting, raving, and threatening his daughter with immediate and violent death, if she refuses to obey him, suddenly appears convinced that he should allow his daughter to marry Felipe, the man she loves.

Not by the force of circumstances or logical plot development does this transpire, but apparently simply by chance. Baltasar had made this decision even before the grotesque Matea appeared to prevent the proposed marriage.

A Madrid me vuelvo, notwithstanding the Moratín influence, either from *El sí de las niñas* or *El barón*, is hardly a dramatic triumph. It is simply a series of scenes written to entertain, but having little dramatic conflict, and that only in the mind of Baltasar. The suggested conflict between Baltasar and his brother Bernardo never materializes, since Baltasar is too easily persuaded of his error. Even Carmen is not acceptable: she is neither too much oppressed on the one hand, nor on the other, independent enough to make her interesting. For the most part, she is very apathetic and uninteresting.

Esteban is, like his mother Matea, a caricature. Bernardo is something of a *raisonneur*, but the play does not stop while he presents moralistic views on the subject of marriage. Without being obtrusive he seems to enjoy some distinction in being the person most responsible for the happy outcome of the "play". But it is not at all effective as drama; there are so many characters entering into it that the purpose or thesis remains obscured.

Bretón wrote voluminously, but in many plays he uses the same framework: a parent, usually the mother, relentlessly trying to marry a daughter to a wealthy man, usually much older than the girl. Circumstances usually require the parent to admit the error, and the girl is left to choose her husband or not, as the case varies in these plays. The plot in each play is often tenuous, slight, even unimportant, and the lesson secondary to it. The interest and usual success of his plays lie in his grotesque characters —usually representing the weakness or vice he wishes to ridicule— and in amusing scenes and situations. His characters, for example, are a Mrs. Malaprop; a woman whose idiosyncracy is sleeping about twenty hours a day; a man who frequently quotes the first half of a familiar proverb and never finishes a sentence; and various rural types —often in outlandish attire— who without exception provoke laughter and are thus objects of ridicule. Lest the viewer miss the point, a *raisonneur* at times points out the moral of the play "con grotesca declamación". In this Moratín still serves as Bretón's model. Examples of these similar plays are *Un novio para la niña, Todo es farsa en este mundo,* and *Dios los cría y ellos se juntan*. The first of these has as its location a boarding house. The landlady tries in many ways to effect matrimony for her daughter, who is betrothed finally not to any of the boarders, but to the man she loves, with her mother's permission, of course. *Todo es farsa en este mundo* is another of the same type, and each of the suitors is a *farsante*, or faker, pretending to be what he is not. Slightly different in theme is *Dios los cría y ellos se juntan*, in which Bretón's thesis is that one should marry within one's own social group, but the idea of our original model *El sí de las niñas* is present as well. With all the comic effects, there is little variety in the plays of Bretón. As Larra points out in a review of the works of Bretón: "Si se ve una de las comedias de Bretón, se ven todas".

To Martínez de la Rosa, Gorostiza, and Bretón de los Herreros, the most important of the continuators of the Moratín tradition, we must add another playwright, Ventura de la Vega (1807-1865), who presented amid his frequent translations several original works, "altas comedias" they have been called, of a *tendencia moralizadora*.

Notable among these was *El hombre de mundo*. This four-act comedy in the Moratinian manner, first presented in 1845, deals with the married life of a *calavera* and preaches the moral that a man cannot lead a dissolute life without suffering the punishment therefor after marriage.

Clara has married Luis, the *hombre de mundo*, reformed, happy in his marriage. Don Juan, an old companion of Luis's in his premarital scrapes, returns from abroad. A conversation with Juan reminds Luis of procedures he employed in his former love schemes, and he begins to suspect his wife. In a complicated series of events in which Clara's younger sister Emilia, Antonio, her *novio*, and don Juan, a roué and *burlador*, are cleverly confused and everyone suspects everyone else, the author succeeds in clearing up all parts of the plot. Suspicious Luis is punished, and the —this time— unsuccessful don Juan has to make a hasty escape.

Among Vega's plays this is the one most completely in the Moratinian tradition: the form is completely neo-classic; the unities are scrupulously observed without straining. Although Moratín had used the traditional division into three acts, it is possible that Vega chose the four-act division to set the play apart from the standard form of the Golden Age *comedia* and the Bretonesque comedy.[2]

The point of departure is the moral precept, and the old but unsurpassed weapon of ridicule is used to drive home the moral lesson. Luis, the rake, although happily married to a virtuous woman, finds the memories of his past adventures rising to destroy his happiness by inspiring him with unfounded jealousy. He becomes a ridiculous figure when he suspects the naive young Antonio, and thus blinded, fails to recognize the real danger of his position. When his wife in turn, through her knowledge of her husband's former escapades, becomes suspicious, the marriage nearly founders. With the emphasis so placed upon the moral issue, the characters, even Luis, lack profundity of delineation and development and are types, rather than individuals.

---

[2] LESLIE, JOHN KENNETH: *Ventura de la Vega and the Spanish Theatre (1820-1865)*, Princeton, 1938.

Menéndez y Pelayo observed in the play less *fuerza cómica* than is to be found in Moratín,[3] and it is indeed true that there is little to be observed in this play of the comic effect produced by doña Irene in *El sí de las niñas*. There is, however, the suave urbanity of what Vega called the "gracia ática".

The greatest weakness in the play is the artificiality of its plot. Too large a part of the action depends upon devices of the comedy of intrigue. Equivocation becomes a mainspring of the plot. But Vega's dramatic talent is manifest in connection with the expected dramatic misunderstandings, for in all of them there is no implausibility. It is a very successful dramatic effort, entertaining while presenting a sound moral lesson.

---

[3] MENÉNDEZ Y PELAYO: *Antología de poetas hispano-americanos* IV, Madrid, 1928, p. 158.

CHAPTER III

TRUTH AND COMMON SENSE

About the year 1850, after Romanticism had run its course, another reaction set in—one that was also to be noted in France. This change was characterized by a greater degree of good taste, measure, and truth in dramatic productions. And yet, even in this period, there was a decided tendency to place upon the stage plays with a moral purpose. Indeed even in France Augier and Dumas *fils* were writing sermons in play form. It was at this moment that two important Spanish dramatists began to write in the same vein—Manuel Tamayo y Baus and Adelardo López de Ayala. These playwrights were attempting to lead the Spanish theater, long monopolized by the romantics, back to truth and common sense. The full credit, however, is due to Tamayo who was the first to open the way for such attempts by replacing verse with prose and applying himself to the study of character.

Tamayo y Baus is generally considered one of the outstanding playwrights of the nineteenth century. Though he did not write as many plays as Bretón de los Herreros, for example, the value of his few contributions to the field of social drama was appreciably greater. Having written several historical plays and at least one classical tragedy *(Virginia)*, he is the dramatist who best represents in the nineteenth century the transition from the romantic and historical theater to social and thesis drama.

Tamayo y Baus wrote only four plays which can be classified as social drama. They are *La bola de nieve* (1856), *Lo positivo* (1862), *Lances de honor* (1863), and *Los hombres de bien* (1870). According to some literary historians, *La bola de nieve* is the first, in point of time, of the modern thesis dramas. It purports to show the unhappy consequences of unreasonable jealousy.

Although Tamayo y Baus wrote much of his work in prose, believing that it could better express his ideas for social improvement, *La bola de nieve* is a three-act verse drama, first presented in the Teatro del Príncipe, May 16, 1856, "a beneficio del primer actor" Joaquín Arjona. The setting for the first and second acts is the country house of a *marqués* near Granada; act three takes place in another *casa de campo* nearby. The time is the 1850's. The role of Fernando was taken by Joaquín Arjona.

Luis, the son of a *marquesa*, is betrothed to María, a young girl brought up by the noble woman in her home; and Clara, the *marquesa*'s daughter, is engaged to Fernando. Unreasonable jealousy in Luis and Clara, especially the latter, soon cause the engagements to be broken. Fernando, in an effort to protect María from Luis's and Clara's unkindness, takes her away with him to another small country place. Luis is so jealous and so infuriated by this action that he provokes Fernando to a duel. Later Luis describes the duel as having taken place, and Fernando is brought in apparently mortally wounded. Luis laments his rashness, and they summon a priest, who marries Fernando and María, leaving Clara and Luis to bewail their unreasonable jealousy and its consequences. Antonio, a doctor-friend of Fernando's, saves his life and pronounces the closing summary:

"Ustedes lo han querido.
Ustedes los han casado."

Valbuena-Prat rates this play above Tamayo's later production *Lo positivo* in regard to the author's *talento escénico*, but has nothing more to say about the play, except that thesis drama in general is "alejado de nuestro gusto". In partial agreement with this critic, it might be said that *La bola de nieve* is not the best of the thesis dramas of the nineteenth century. The thesis is flimsy, and Tamayo y Baus has warped characters and situations to defend it. Both Clara and Luis are so unreasonably jealous that this failing appears a mania, indeed in Clara's personality, a definite derangement, for it is really her influence over her brother Luis which leads him to provoke the duel with Fernando. Yet she is not mad. This is a precarious situation then, because her actions and comments are so peculiar that an audience might misconstrue them and regard them as laughable, although the intent is not comedy.

As is frequently the case with thesis plays, dramatic force is lost from the warping of the characters to develop the thesis. María and Fernando are too good to be true, while Clara and Luis are so despicable in every way that we wonder how Fernando and María could ever have become engaged to them. Clara searches Fernando's clothes for *billets doux* she has no reason to expect to find. While professing his devotion to María, Luis makes love to Juana the maid and then mistreats her husband. These are but two examples of their exaggeratedly base character.

To effect his purpose, Tamayo had to force the "snowball" idea, despite its potential as a thesis. Though this is an obvious weakness, the author's stage experience enabled him to bring the play to its dénouement interestingly enough. The monotony of the incidents provoked by Clara's extreme jealousy is relieved by humorous verses and slapstick comedy provided by the servants Juana and Pedro. Because of the universality of jealousy *La bola de nieve* is not localized or "dated", and could be presented today. But, in spite of its good points, the play is not sound. Only an excellent interpretation of the various roles by superior actors and actresses at the *estreno* could have kept it on the boards.

The usual device of chance meetings and mistaken identities add to the complication of the plot. Several scenes have nothing to with the main action, and could be omitted with no loss to the play. The roles of Antonio and the *marquesa* are of only slight importance. Antonio, a doctor, justifies his presence in saving Fernando's life at the end of the play. But the *marquesa* serves only as *confidante*, a person one may "have to see" when the author needs to remove one of the characters from the stage for a time.

It would seem that here Tamayo y Baus did not have enough material for a full-length play. Antonio and the *marquesa*, supernumeraries both, were added to the work only as dramatic potentialities, which, in the final analysis, do not contribute to the effectiveness of the drama. The thesis is far-fetched. The solution of the play and punishment seem forced, and the marriage of

Fernando and María as he lies at death's door, is anticlimatic, romantic, sentimental, out of place, even maudlin.

The closing lines are intended to serve as a reminder to the audience of the subject (jealousy) and purpose of the play, and as a clincher for Tamayo's argument. Yet they fail in this intent, hardly producing the tears perhaps expected from the audience. It would seem that Tamayo's purpose in these lines was to indicate that as a result of their jealousy, Clara and Luis have caused Fernando and María to be married, and that this result is unfortunate, when it is not. María and Fernando were in love and should have married. So this couplet is misleading, empty, and merely rhetorical.

In making these observations it must be understood that the author leads the reader to believe that Fernando is to recover from the wound he received in the duel with Luis. The drama would be more effective as stark tragedy, that is, if Fernando were to die.

About the middle of the nineteenth century Dumas *fils* wrote a play called *La Question d'argent,* first presented in 1857. And it was not long thereafter that Tamayo y Baus wrote his money play, *Lo positivo.* This three-act *comedia* in prose was first presented (under the name of Joaquín Estébañez, October 25, 1862. In a "nota del autor" we learn that *Lo positivo* is an "imitación de la que escribió en francés Leon Laya con el título de *Le Duc Job* (1859). La significación del pensamiento moral que entraña el asunto aparece tal vez más concreta, más clara y viva en la obra española que en la francesa".

The plot of *Lo positivo* is somewhat more complicated than *La bola de nieve.* After long absence Rafael returns to marry Cecilia only to find her betrothed to a rich South American. Formerly wealthy, Rafael, having given all his money to a friend, is now poor. But, he continues his suit and seems about to win Cecilia. She, however, influenced by her father, decides in favor of the rich South American. The news comes that the South American is to marry another. At last, somewhat influenced by a friend's very happy marriage with, like Rafael, a poor man, Cecilia decides to marry Rafael, who in the nick of time, unexpectedly receives all his money from the friend to whom he had loaned it long before.

Tamayo's thesis seems to be twofold: first, that one should marry for love, not money; and a minor thesis, secondary to the other, that of *El sí de las niñas,* that a young girl deserves the right to choose her own husband, although the latter point is not stressed. As to the first thesis, the author formulates a mild attack on the money-worship of the mid-nineteenth century, a fertile field popular with *dramaturgos* of other countries as well. Many Spanish playwrights of this period seem to have followed at least in part the pattern of social comedy set by the French leaders Dumas *fils* and Émile Augier. At this time (1820-1865) there was much of the French drama on the Spanish stage. Indeed many of the most prominent Spanish playwrights resorted to translation from the French as a wellpaid source of livelihood.

The playwrights discussed heretofore have presented the thesis or thesis element through a *raisonneur* or through the logical development of the lesson in the plot, the moral to be deduced from either or both of these. In *Lo positivo,* however, a verbal debate occurs between Pablo, representing *lo positivo,* and the *marqués,* who defends the traditional custom or marrying for love. As will be observed, the actors must have been exceptionally proficient at this point in the play if interest in such a long harangue or debates was to be maintained. Perhaps audiences were patient while these two antagonists faced each other for a few minutes of hotly contested oratory, and the play stopped. As to the protagonists in the play, Rafael and Cecilia, they are almost pawns in this struggle. They become marionettes manipulated by the author to state and develop his thesis. Neither has much character or personality.

The *marqués* is the *raisonneur,* stopping the play on several occasions to present the ideas of the author. Also, as a melodramatic touch, an unexpected letter appears, and becomes a strong factor in making Cecilia determine to marry Rafael. The action of the play is delayed while she sentimentally declares the contents of the letter, in which an old friend advises her to marry, but only for love. The lesson, or thesis, is quite clear.

Yet, in spite of all these external devices used by Tamayo y Baus to express his opinion on the subject of marriage for money, a practice which must have been fairly prevalent to make the author feel that it warranted corrective measures, the play, discounting the obvious and uncanny timing of important events and expected or fortunate-and-unexpected occurrences, is interesting enough dramatically, not because of the characterization, however, but because of Tamayo's well-known "arte escénico", though it does not reach its culmination in *Lo positivo*.

As usual, characterization suffers, while the author develops his thesis, contrasting the group of characters advocating the thesis and those who were militant against it. Though Pablo, unlike Clara and Luis in *La bola de nieve,* is not vicious, he is determined in his effort to marry Cecilia to the rich South American, which suggests the *El sí de las niñas* theme.

Cecilia, Rafael, and the *marqués*, the opposing faction, are not realistic characters. Cecilia is the best delineated of these. When she is to marry the rich man, she wavers between *Lo positivo* and love; then she declares she will marry for love, becoming romantic and normal in the final analysis; but the gesture of disposing of her wealth by giving it to her brother so that he may marry Matilde (these two never appear) strains credibility. Furthermore, Rafael is too generous, too lavish in his philanthropy, so rare an individual that, looking at the situation realistically, he hardly seems a good match for Cecilia or anyone. Obviously, Tamayo's description of Rafael's complete unconcern for money is the author's way of attacking worship of money. But in this incident Rafael turns out to be puerile, a playboy in his abnormal disregard for this world's goods, whereas Tamayo's purpose was simply to show Rafael's generosity. As has been noted, the *marqués* while serving as *raisonneur*, is important to the plot in that it is he who persuades Pablo to relent in his campaign to force Cecilia to marry Muñoz, the rich man.

Although Valbuena-Prat does not regard *Lo positivo* or any thesis drama as enjoyable, it no doubt had some value for the time it was presented. Apparently Tamayo y Baus was conscious of the prevailing conditions in Spain and was much concerned about them. Certainly in *Lo positivo* he makes a good case against the custom of marriage for the sole purpose of financial betterment.

Soon after the appearance of *Lo positivo,* Tamayo y Baus presented another play on social consciousness, *Lances de honor.* In this three-act *comedia* in prose, first presented in the Teatro del Circo, September 1, 1863, the author states that the action covers only four hours.

Paulino and Miguel have long been close friends. But over government policy their fathers, Villena and Fabián, respectively, become so insulting in their debate in the Cámara de Diputados that in accordance with the custom of the times, a duel must be fought. It is Fabián's prerogative to challenge, but as he is a sincere Christian gentleman, though known to be brave too, he refuses. When Villena challenges him he at first refuses, but is forced into the duel by Fabián's provocation. In an argument which arose during their heated discussion of the imminent conflict, Villena's son, Paulino, feeling honor-bound to observe the criminal convention, challenges Miguel, and they go off to duel at once with pistols. On hearing of this unexpected development, Villena, Fabián, and Candelaria (Miguel's mother) hasten to try to prevent the duel, but arrive too late. Miguel is dying, and Paulino, who had regarded the duel as little more than a sporting event, suddenly becomes aware of its grim significance. Miguel forgives both the grief-stricken boy and Villena, who had been so insistent that the social amenities be observed to the letter. He dies victim of the barbaric custom.

Though dueling in the United States was restricted to hot-bloods in the South, in Spain, or more probably in Madrid, Seville, and some of the larger cities, it may have been more general, an even more disturbing social evil. At least it had reached such proportions that Tamayo deemed it worthy of his special attention. Even Valbuena-Prat says the play had a "valor de época".

Lances de honor is a true thesis drama, sober, didactic—an impressive attack on dueling. In a logical, fateful, and inexorable manner events lead on to the ultimate tragic conclusion. Dramatically speaking, this is an improvement over Tamayo's earlier thesis plays. The characters are, in the main, more normal, and only slightly strained to emphasize the thesis. Situation and action are more skillfully and effectively handled, showing the attitude of society toward the idea of personal honor and the duel as the only manner of preserving it in nineteenth-century Spain. Indeed, it is not the characters who are warped to present the thesis: it was the society which had such an attitude toward this criminal custom that was distorted. It recalls *pundonor* and the "capa y espada" plays of the Golden Age. The play is really an effective argument against the deplorable practice. Indicative of Tamayo's understanding of the dueling problem, and to point out the extent to which the foolish code had gone, one of the minor characters says, "Las ofensas tienen mayor o menor gravedad, según vale más o menos la persona que las recibe".

As the author had done in *Lo positivo*, he has included in the *dramatis personae* a *raisonneur*, Candelaria, Miguel's mother, a novel addition, because in other plays the *raisonneurs* have been men, not women. Through the logical development of the plot, and through her clear, carefully drawn characterization Tamayo presents his moral lesson. However, the play loses much of its dramatic force in the fiery sermon of Candelaria which is used to develop the thesis and the attitude of the church toward dueling—a somewhat fond and unsophisticated manner of attacking the problem.

The play is an improvement over Tamayo's earlier dramas for its dramatic interest, and perhaps the most striking characteristic of *Lances de honor* is the irresistible momentum of convention leading to inevitable tragedy. This force is ever-present before the reader, present in all its cruelty, yet apparently unassailable in its position in civilized society. Tamayo's success in describing and developing the grim aspects of the awful hold this custom must have had on Madrid society is impressive.

As to character-delineation and development, all the characters are effectively presented. Fabián and Candelaria are especially good characterizations. She strives to prevent the duel between Villena and her husband, but the custom has grown too strong, and he is forced to yield to its inexorable power. But the real tragedy is in Paulino's murder of his erstwhile friend Miguel. Paulino was, like his father, Villena, a blind slave to observance of an insane custom, and he is crushed in his guilt and remorse at the tragic climax of the play. Even the servants, notably Bernabé, Fabián's valet, like their masters imbued with respect for the idea of *pundonor*, hasten the dread catastrophe.

In spite of some weaknesses, *Lances de honor* is a successful combination of the drama and the thesis. It was not necessary for Tamayo to force the characters to present the moral lesson as much as in his earlier plays. And Candelaria, though conspicuous as the *raisonneur*, plays an essential role in the drama as adviser and moral support to Fabián, the protagonist.

One of the most significant of the dramatic works of Tamayo y Baus, significant, perhaps, in a manner hardly anticipated by the author, as will be seen later, was *Los hombres de bien*. This three-act drama in prose was first presented December 17, 1870. The scene is Lorenzo's *casa de campo*, and the time 1870.

Three "hombres de bien" (which, in the case of this drama, is an ironic phrase meaning just the opposite of "honorable men"), a Conde, Juanito, and Lorenzo, deplore the evils of society, wishing someone would do something to correct the situation, mentioning in particular a certain Leandro Quiroga as a scoundrel, atheist, reprobate, and menace to society. When he enters, uninvited, they treat him as they might a most respected friend, fawning on him in a shameful manner. Lorenzo's daughter Adelaida loves Quiroga, and he wants her to run away with him. Quiroga tries to seduce Andrea, daughter of a paralytic living nearby. The Conde and Juanito appear and do nothing to punish him, considering it an affair unworthy of their attention as "hombres de bien". Damián, Lorenzo's slightly crippled secretary (with no social position to maintain, hence able to condescend to help a girl in distress), protects Andrea against Quiroga, and for his efforts, is thrown out of Lorenzo's house. Quiroga, having become unbearable in his insulting, high-handed manner, has to be bribed by Lorenzo before he will consent to leave Lorenzo's house, but he boasts that he will take Adelaida with him. Still Lorenzo, the Conde, and Juanito do nothing to punish this criminal. When Damián fights Quiroga in a vain attempt to protect Andrea, the cripple is wounded. Andrea rushes into Lorenzo's house seeking his protection, and amid the excitement this "hombre de bien" suddenly realizes that Adelaida is missing and that Quiroga has taken her away with him.

The thesis is that excessive tolerance, based on little faith or on complete lack of faith in anything, especially toleration of dishonesty in people of position (like Quiroga), is as criminal as or worse than recognized crime itself. Damián, who acts as *raisonneur*, a voice crying in the wilderness, laments the existence of these "hombres de bien" for their lack of faith in anything; they have no convictions or creed and condone any kind of vice, excusing themselves by saying as honorable men that they must have nothing to do with that kind of men, preferring to act like ostriches, pretending not to see the evil going on about them. Damián even compares them to Pilate, in their refusing to accept responsibility. Quiroga himself, depicted as the worst of men, guilty of every crime, completely amoral, rather than immoral, on being chided by Adelaida for his wickedness, says, "Piensa qué es peor: si creer a medias o no creer". Quiroga believes himself better, or at least more honest (the author's ideas too?) than the Conde, Juanito, and Lorenzo and their tolerance based on little faith.

In this play the chief weakness is that common to many thesis plays: the play is subordinated to the thesis, the characters reduced to puppets, mouthpieces for the author's ideas. Poor, long-suffering, patient, honorable, brave Damián, with no social standing among these overbred but spineless men, though a cripple, alone stands up to the uninvited guest Quiroga. He reproaches these "honorable men" for allowing such men as Quiroga to remain free to practice their wickedness instead of making an effort, as Damián does, to teach them a lesson.

To assure the effectiveness of the moral lesson, to show the possible consequences of excessive tolerance, really apathy, Lorenzo —the weakest, yet the leader of the three men— is made the victim of his own cowardly character, when Adelaida runs away with Quiroga. Her character is explained by the author's reference to the type of reading she does—broad for a girl of her day, the inference being that her father should have been more concerned with his daughter's upbringing than he seems to have been. Though it is not clearly stated, it seems that Tamayo indicates that she was not forced to go away with Quiroga, but that she went of her own free will, ill-tutored and misled.

Though the drama is weakened by the forced presentation of the thesis, *Los hombres de bien* did not escape notice, and indeed may have had some influence on Spanish society in 1870, because, according to Hurtado y González Palencia, in their *Historia de la literatura española*, this "sátira dramática contra las tolerancias con que la sociedad mira a personajes indignos... atrajo sobre Tamayo ciertas censuras de elementos de ideas diferentes y el autor resolvió no escribir más para el teatro", devoting himself to his duties as "secretario perpetuo" to the Academy, and to his work as director of the National Library until his death in 1898.

Reviewing the works of Tamayo, we observe that the author's theses and ideas are strikingly different from those of previous playwrights who wrote thesis plays or plays with a "thesis element". From the plays by Moratín with emphasis on the moral aspects of certain customs, notably education of young girls, the thesis play was gradually assuming new characteristics, and the *dramaturgos* of the mid-nineteenth century were treating different subjects in varying ways. In the works of Tamayo on the effects of jealousy *(La bola de nieve)*, the money question *(Lo positivo)*, dueling *(Lances de honor)*, and apathy toward social conditions *(Los hombres de bien)*, greater emphasis is being placed on larger, less restricted problems of society. The whole idea of the thesis play was growing.

Contemporary with Tamayo y Baus was Adelardo López de Ayala. While writing more, Ayala's dramatic skill was better developed, representing the highest attainments of the *alta comedia* in the nineteenth century. His first play to come under consideration here is *El tejado de vidrio*. This four-act *comedia* in verse was presented in 1857. The scene is Mariano's house.

Mariano wonders why his wife's relative Julia, who lives with them, does not go out much socially. Unknown to them is the fact that Julia and a Conde de Laurel have been secretly married for a year, the marriage being kept secret lest the Conde's uncle terminate his allowance. Julia is afraid that someone will suspect something and think their relationship immoral. She wants to announce that their marriage has taken place, saying:

> "Me va causando rubor
> Dar al legítimo amor
> Las apariencias del vicio."

The Conde, on the other hand, is still a would-be Casanova, trying to make love to Dolores, Mariano's wife, all the time advising Carlos, a young protege of his, how to court a girl of whom Carlos is very fond. She, of course, is Julia. Dolores tells Julia of the Conde's interest in her, which makes Julia, her jealousy aroused, determine to seek revenge. So she pretends to give encouragement to Carlos, though remaining honorable. Dolores, also still honorable, decides to leave Madrid for a while to shun this temptation, and she writes a note to the Conde telling him her plans. Too late she realizes this was unwise, for Mariano may find the note. Carlos in his excitement reveals the identity of his love for Julia to the Conde, her husband, who shows no surprise, only asks to be allowed to listen in on their next meeting. Before it begins, however, the Conde enters, meets Julia, confesses to his extramarital activity, begs forgiveness, and seems repentant for his misdeeds. Mariano finds Dolores's note, but the still smooth Conde explains it all away, and declares he is Julia's husband. So at last they are going to live as husband and wife; Mariano's and Dolores's marriage is preserved, and Carlos goes abroad.

The thesis is suggested by the title, namely the old proverb, "People who live in glass houses should not throw stones", or as Hurtado y González Palencia more eruditely state, "Muchas veces el vicio y el escándalo se vuelven contra el vicioso". The Conde, having been *mujeriego* for so long, cannot relinquish his premarital, bachelor habits, and continues to pursue the ladies, though he is now married. In this pursuit he exposes himself and his wife to slander, in her case undeserved. For any of several reasons, therefore, he needs a lesson. It is not necessary for the playwright to force the plot to point up the thesis, which is usually the case in the plays of Tamayo y Baus. And the play comes out the better for it. Ayala's characters are not forced and there is no *raisonneur* who stops the play to expound on Ayala's social ideas.

A new note appears in this play by Ayala, irony, a quality heretofore lacking in the plays studied. The author purports to teach a lesson, of course, and he attacks prevailing social attitudes as he does in these lines spoken by Julia, at last aware of her husband's extramarital love pursuits, in Act III:

> A él (Conde)... todo el mundo a él
> Le festeja y aun le envidia,
> Y dan gloria, sí, señor,
> Estas hazañas gentiles.

Julia is not the *raisonneur*. It is logical and in keeping with the scene, the action, and the plot for her to make these pertinent remarks, which at the same time reflect the author's ideas on certain weaknesses in Spanish society in the mid-nineteenth century.

There are weaknesses in the play which should be criticized. When Carlos shows the Conde a letter written to him by Julia, the Conde does not recognize his wife's handwriting! And, to the disappointment of the reader, the Carlos (pupil) and Conde (teacher) situation is artificial and does not come off well in the "big" scene. Carlos seems about to succeed in winning the favors of his preceptor's wife, and he even challenges the Conde to a duel, unaware of the relationship of Julia and the Conde and believing that the Conde is trying to win Julia too. This is the big scene of the play when "el vicio y el escándalo se vuelven al vicioso". But this scene seems too contrived. The duel is not fought; the Conde's "punishment" seems too light. This is characteristic of the tone of Ayala's plays, one of the differentiating factors in his and Tamayo's works. There is no violence in the play. The tone is urbane, polished, sophisticated throughout.

In most of the technical aspects of the play Ayala shows himself to be as clever a *dramaturgo* as Tamayo. Like Tamayo's successful dramatic efforts, however, Ayala's play depends heavily on chance and fortunate concurrence of people and events to bring about the desired or feared actions. These chance occurrences are not always satisfactorily explained to the reader, though they must inevitably be accepted as essential to dramatic technique.

In this play one dramatic device resorted to in the extreme is eavesdropping on all sides. This device almost destroys every character. Indeed, we find no lofty and unforgettable characters in *El tejado de vidrio*. All five principal characters are run-of-the-mill, ordinary individuals, but hardly "types" in the pejorative sense of the word. They are merely uninspired.

The plot, however, is nicely complicated, well-suited in its involutions to present the author's thesis. *El tejado de vidrio*, though a serious play, has a lighter tone than the pointed, weighty works of Tamayo y Baus. The thesis does not keep the play from being amusing and entertaining.

Like Tamayo, Ayala wrote a money play: *El tanto por ciento*. This three-act *comedia* in verse was first presented in the Teatro del Príncipe May 18, 1861. The scene of the first and second acts is a resort on the Cantabrian coast. Act three takes place in Madrid.

Petra, Gaspar, Andrés, and Roberto, who seems to be the leader of the group, are interested in buying lands which Pablo, a good friend of theirs owns, because they have information that a new canal will be built through the property. Pablo, though unaware of this, needs money to finance a villa he has just bought for Isabel, his *novia*, a countess, also known to the people mentioned, from whom they hope to borrow money. Roberto tells Pablo he will lend him the money, Pablo putting up his land for collateral. The money Pablo expected to receive from business transactions does not come, the day arrives when he must repay the loan, and it seems that Roberto will receive the valuable property. A conspiracy to make Pablo suspect Isabel of immorality with Andrés is staged in an attempt to destroy Pablo's love for Isabel. But, at the moment when all looks black for Pablo, money with which to repay Roberto's loan arrives, put up by Isabel.

Ayala's thesis is that people will do anything for money. The attack is mild, but dramatically set forth: an attack ostensibly against quick-riches schemes. But the underlying aim of the playwright is to point out the more philosophical thesis. This is done in the normal development of the plot, though a *raisonneur* appears in, of all people, Roberto, when he acknowledges his ulterior motives in lending Pablo the money, having involved others in his scheme, intending to use them, then to cheat them as he would have done to Pablo, if it should have become necessary for the furtherance of his own aims. He himself declares:

> Todo se da a Belcebú
> Cuando media el interés.
>> Act III, scene XIII

The thesis, however, is presented in the natural outcome of the play. The plot is simple, not too involved, depending on chance and fortunate timing. There are incidents described in detail suggesting motives, actions, events, which seem to have little bearing on the plot or the thesis, such as Petra's conceit in believing Pablo loves her; the inclusion of Andrés as a possible seducer of Isabel; and the long account which follows in explanation of his visit to her room.

Though there are too many characters in this play —Andrés, Petra, and Gaspar are unimportant— all are portrayed as greedy money-grabbers. None, moreover, seems overemphasized to suit the plot or to point up the thesis. Similar to Tamayo's *Lo positivo* on the theme of the money problem, *El tanto por ciento* is a reflection of Ayala's attitude toward greed and the apparent lack of business ethics in nineteenth-century Spain. At any rate, he makes an interesting play from the elements he uses, combining cleverly the plot and the thesis.

The Don Juan theme has long appealed to Spanish playwrights, and, with a new approach Ayala wrote *El nuevo don Juan*. This three-act *comedia* in verse was first presented in the Teatro del Circo in 1863. "La acción es contemporánea y dura menos de veinticuatro horas", says a "nota del autor". Does this note show a serious concern for observance of the unities as late as the 1860's?

Diego and Elena his wife return home from mass, he having noticed a man staring at her. Diego becomes suspicious, having been something of a Don Juan himself. She explains that the man must have been looking at Paulina, their neighbor. Soon afterward, the stranger, Don Juan de Alvarado, boldly enters their home, claiming to bring a letter from her mother. The letter, read later by Diego, reveals that, as Diego had suspected, Don Juan seeks Elena's love. Paulina declares to Elena that she loves Juan. Of course, Juan is interested only in Elena, but accepts the role of Paulina's suitor imposed on him by Diego, in order to go on seeing Elena. After a series of chance meetings, mistaken identities, and much letter-writing, Don Juan's real interest and intentions are discovered, he is humiliated by Diego, and has to leave Diego's home. Paulina is cured of her passion and learns what it took all of them a long time to learn: never trust a Don Juan.

This is a very mild attack on Don Juanism, and the weak thesis is not developed realistically enough. Incidents abound, but they are carelessly introduced and developed. The letter hoax on which Don Juan obtains an audience with Elena is flimsy, a chance occurrence depending on a slim possibility, a coincidence of events and in all most unlikely. A successful Don Juan would have employed a more sophisticated, less naive kind of ruse to enter the home of a woman whom he wished to seduce.

Then too, Diego's inane, childish, unmanly reaction to this situation, on learning of Don Juan's purpose in coming to his home, weakens the force of the play. It cannot be that Ayala simply wanted to give a new twist to the old jealous husband-surprised lover situation. Diego's capricious intent to play along with the plans of Don Juan to seduce his wife in the manner of the cat playing with the mouse is not natural. A man would have taken more violent, more immediate action. The play loses force here. In fact, motivating force is noticeably absent in *El nuevo don Juan*. Also the plan Diego has to invite Don Juan to his home, there to ridicule him publicly before guests at the expense of his wife's reputation is wholly unacceptable. The coolest of husbands would not have resorted to such elaborate preparations as these. Why didn't Diego simply eject this don Juan at once and ignore the incident? It seems unnaturally forced in an attempt to provide dramatic situations and interest. Therefore, it is not effective in presentation.

Another shortcoming in the author's dramatic technique seems present in his attempt to punish Don Juan as one might a little boy. Such a scene is carefully planned by Diego, but never takes place. After all the time spent in discussion of the ruse, a glaring weakness lies in its not taking place. At the end of Act II the would-be lover is made to appear ridiculous when Diego encloses Don Juan in a large *armario* for the night, again a punishment which might be meted out to an unruly adolescent, hardly the way for men to treat men. The recurrence of incidents of this type would seem to indicate that Ayala intended in this manner, by exposing the guilty party —here the would-be lover— to the grossest ridicule, to give fitting punishment to a Don Juan. But the tone of the piece in most of the scenes is hardly in keeping with the slapstick resolution of the plot.

Though over-complicated, this play affords humorous and entertaining scenes. The lesson is so unobtrusive that it could have gone unnoticed by some and must have had very little effect on the audience's *mores.*

A much better play than *El nuevo don Juan* was *Consuelo,* the best of Ayala's plays, in three acts and in verse, first presented some fifteen years afterward, in 1878, at the Teatro Español.

Consuelo is a beautiful young girl who loves Fernando, and he loves her. But Consuelo plans to marry Ricardo, feeling that his greater wealth will enable her to live as she would like to. Fernando is a capable, ambitious, honest young man who is doing well in his own work, but Consuelo wants more than that now. So she marries Ricardo. He soon finds a mistress, Abela. To try to make Ricardo jealous and so return to her, Consuelo writes a note to Fernando which she hopes Ricardo will read, asking Fernando to come to see her. Contrary to her expectations, Fernando receives the letter and he goes at once to Consuelo's house. She is worried lest her husband find Fernando with her, and she orders him to leave. Ricardo returns home to tell her that he must go to Paris on business. She accuses him of infidelity. He ignores her complaints and leaves for Paris, with Abela, of course. At this point the maid enters to tell her that her mother has just died. Her death leaves Consuelo completely alone with all the wealth she coveted, but with no one to love her.

Consuelo is a good thesis play, in which the author contends that marriage for money is a dangerous risk and that marriage should be contracted for love only. To prove his thesis Ayala sets up a plausible situation and a convincing argument. And one of the most admirable features of the *comedia* is the scarcity of nonessential material. The play moves in a straight line without the slightest suggestion of false leads or of padding. The necessary minor threads of plot are deftly brought into the main skein. By way of example, Consuelo's mother's heart ailment is made known early enough to prepare the audience for the announcement of her death.

The character-delineation is excellent. As is usually the case, however, with thesis plays even the best characterizations are somewhat overdrawn to point up the thesis. But this defect is held to a minimum in *Consuelo.* Consuelo's failing, her excessive fondness for this world's goods, is her only fault. There is no illusion to an immoral life. Indeed, the incident of the letter to

Fernando has as its reason for presentation an attempt to win back her husband. She, then, is excellently portrayed, a pathetic, pitiable creature. Ricardo and the minor characters are reasonable. But Fernando could never have married Consuelo. He is perhaps too good for her, too perfect for anyone. Though characterization is generally good, and in keeping with the tone of the play, Fernando is not a person one could expect to meet very often.

The moral lesson is presented in the natural outcome of the play. Ayala does not include a *raisonneur*. In this respect the play is an improvement on most thesis plays, because the action is rapid, never stopping while the author points out the moral lesson or his thesis. Indeed, Fernando is cleverly brought back into the picture near the middle of the piece for the audience, and for Consuelo —to her chagrin— to see how well he has succeeded in business. In her vanity and greedy ambitions Consuelo "queda castigada".

The above phrase is really significant because Consuelo learns her lesson painfully and irrevocably. The satire contained in these two words "queda castigada" is mordant, grim, final. As has been mentioned earlier, this satirical, ironical note is a comparatively new one in social drama in the nineteenth century. Earlier authors had seen fit to teach through ridicule; Ayala himself, in *El nuevo don Juan* had tried to present his thesis through preaching; and in other plays through plots containing moral lessons. Ayala's sophisticated play *Consuelo* presents in a tone of satire a lesson destined for an audience in great part composed of representative members of the very social class he associates with the money question.

One example of the satire in the play is found in a conversation between Fernando and an old "friend", Fulgencio, who had offered Fernando quick riches in a not entirely unquestionable business deal. Fulgencio is berating him for his foolishness in not taking advantage of this offer, and Fernando replies apparently voicing the author's observation or opinion on society in the 1860-1870 period as follows:

> Simple, tonto, majadero...
> Es el premio que hoy anima
> Al hombre que más estima
> Su conciencia que el dinero.

One critic, Suárez Bravo, quoted in an article in the Espasa Enciclopedia, has said, "No he leído sátira más honda que *Consuelo* contra los vicios sociales".

In the first part of Ayala's dramatic production his interest lay notably in the traditional theater, recalling the works of Calderón. He added life and vigor to Spanish drama, and with him modern social conditions and contemporary Spanish life enter into the Spanish dramatic field. With *El tejado de vidrio, El tanto por ciento, El nuevo don Juan,* and *Consuelo* Ayala rises to the front rank in the modern comedy of character and the psychological and social drama. In these four plays Ayala is at his best, and the fundamental principle underlying his dramatic talents is easily discernible in each one. The punishment of the sins of modern society seems to be his first dramatic principle.

Contributing much to the Spanish stage both in the field of historical drama written for the edification of the public and, more successfully, in various socio-moral dramas attacking social customs in need of correction was Luis de Eguílaz (1830-1874). Though he belonged to the same school as Ayala, the difference between them is mainly one of character and talent. Eguílaz was a man of letters, and nothing more; Ayala was a man of the world, a journalist, deputy, minister after the revolution of 1801 and again under the Restoration, President of the *Congreso*, orator, and poet.

Writing as a young man, Eguílaz made his first claim to fame with *Verdades amargas.* This three-act *comedia* in verse was first presented at the Teatro de Variedades January 20, 1853. The scene for Act One is Sevilla; the other acts take place in Madrid.

Wealthy Félix is interested in helping Luis, his daughter Margarita's *novio*, and he has been successful in having him elected *diputado* from Sevilla. But, as Luis rises to greater power and position he forgets his benefactors. Carlos, a young man for whom Félix has founded a newspaper business, in order that the new editor (Carlos) may assist Luis in his career, turns against him and thus prevents him from being reelected minister. Faithful Félix arranges Luis's reinstatement by royal decree, however, in spite of the latter's apparent disdain for his former *novia* and forgetfulness of her father's aid. Luis, at last conscious of his debt to them, renounces the proffered restoration, forsakes politics, and returns to Margarita.

Eguílaz's thesis is that ambitious people soon forget obligations to their benefactors. The author establishes a good case for this premise, proving that

> "Cuando se logra subir
> No se piensa en la escalera."
> Act. II, Scene IV

Though the frame or plot of this play is sound, it remains a frame upon which Eguílaz hangs many moral observations, and the play stops frequently for him to pronounce his *verdades amargas*. Acknowledging the growing power of the press, Eguílaz says, in the person of Félix:

> "Ella sola en nuestra edad
> De dar renombre se encarga.
> Es una verdad amarga,
> Pero es una gran verdad."
> Act. I, Scene III

And Félix adds, referring to Luis's rapid advancement and his own help to him channeled through Carlos's newspaper editorials, "Jamás hay hombre sin hombre" (behind him). These are but two of many such observations of Eguílaz, the homely philosopher. In spite of frequent delays in action, the play has considerable dramatic interest in the development and description of Luis's meteoric rise. Eguílaz, however, destroys the effectiveness of the play in the weak ending, having Luis repent and return to his *novia*. It would have been much more effective a conclusion if the author had permitted Luis to marry Hortensia, win the election, and forget his benefactors completely. (Hortensia is Margarita's rival for Luis's affection.) Instead the play has a Hollywood-type dénouement, hence, both thesis and play lose force.

Written the same year as *Verdades amargas* was Eguílaz's second play *Las prohibiciones*, a three-act *comedia* in verse first presented at the Teatro del Príncipe, October 20, 1853. The scene is Madrid.

Gonzalo and Victor are ambitious young writers, but neither is very successful. Gonzalo's book *Historia del porvenir* has not sold well, and Cristóbal, a newspaper editor, is about to fire Victor, his ghost-writer. Fernando and Gabriel are Gonzalo's rich uncles; the former fears that Gonzalo's radical book will hurt the family name, and —to keep an eye on him— suggests that it would be advisable for Gonzalo to live with him. This is fortunate because Fernando's niece and ward, Carolina, who lives at the home of Fernando, and Gonzalo are in love. Gabriel has arranged to have Gonzalo's book banned for a time to insure its success later. Cristóbal, the editor, complicating matters further, is trying to marry Carolina. Gonzalo is so worried about this and about his book, that he is planning to commit suicide. But, Gabriel talks him out of the notion. Gabriel is in danger of imprisonment because of the radical ideas expressed in his book, but Carolina uses her friends' political influence to save him, and Gonzalo, his book now about to sell through the efforts of Gabriel, can marry Carolina.

In almost the same manner employed in *Verdades amargas* Eguílaz uses a weakly-constructed plot to provide a frame upon which to present his ideas on education. He is notably unsuccessful in combining these two entities—the plot and his social observations. The outcome of the play has little to do with the recommendations he suggests in passing.

The thesis seems to be that young people should not be peremptorily prohibited (hence the title) from developing their abilities according to their natural inclinations. He probably intended to include in this play the idea of competent guidance as provided by Gabriel, the *raisonneur*. In contrast with Gabriel is the character of Fernando, the stern guardian who prohibits Carolina from going out, and Gonzalo from visiting his home lest his wife be corrupted by him; he even prohibits Gonzalo from continuing his efforts to sell his book. In support of the idea of the "prohibiciones" Cristóbal is particularly demanding in the case of Victor's normal self-expression. Yet, though Gabriel does what he can to advance the sale of Gonzalo's book and to assist him in his courtship of Carolina, his chief role is that of the *raisonneur*. His lines are evidently greatly increased in number because the role was played by a leading actor of his day, Joaquín Arjona; and, probably, to fill out an otherwise short second act.

It is apparent that Eguílaz thought of himself as teacher as well as playwright, because he cannot refrain from presenting a moral lesson or observation on little or no provocation. He does bring out that restrictions or "prohibiciones" serve frequently to make what is banned appear attractive and thus, they could be dangerous. The graphic example of Gonzalo's book being banned to increase interest in it attests to this.

Of especial interest among the characters is Gonzalo, in that he really recalls the romantic hero. His home in the garret; everything he wants or tries to do seems doomed to failure or disappointment; he has a misunderstanding with his uncle Fernando, who reaches the point of making him leave his house; and at the tragic climax, Gonzalo is about to commit suicide. Unlike the characters of *Verdades amargas* these characters do not seem distorted for emphasis. Only Fernando seems forced for effect in his characterization representing "prohibiciones".

One of the most sentimental of the works of Eguílaz was *La cruz del matrimonio*. This three-act *comedia* in verse was first presented at the Teatro de Variedades, November 28, 1861. The scene is Madrid in 1860.

Two couples, Enriqueta and Manuel, and Mercedes and Félix, have been married three years. The husbands continue to lead a gay life, often leaving their wives alone. But Enriqueta, instead of caring for her children, tries to satisfy her longing for affection and companionship by going out as much as her husband does, while Mercedes is the loyal stay-at-home. Even though the son of Mercedes and Félix is desperately ill, Félix, Manuel, and Enriqueta attend a grand ball. Félix returns home —Mercedes hopes because of their sick son— only to borrow money from her with which to gamble. Manuel announces that in a duel he has just killed Alfredo, who had been paying too much attention to his wife at the ball. This news and Félix's now growing concern for his wife and son combine to make him realize what a *cruz* Mercedes has borne; he repents of his *calaveradas*, and their marriage is saved. But, as a result of Enriqueta's and Manuel's selfish actions and especially of her reactions to his nocherniego habits, which ultimately were the cause of Alfredo's death, they must separate because Manuel, a murderer, will have to flee for his life.

The thesis is that a woman's place is in the home, as the familiar Spanish proverb says:

> "La mujer casada,
> La pierna quebrada
> y en casa."

Yet the treatment given this thesis does not constitute a very strong defense of matrimony—rather does Eguílaz paint a poor picture of it. Apparently marriage has little to recommend it. It is a "cross" consisting of misunderstandings, selfishness, support of the double standard of morality, and eternal waiting on the part of the loyal wife for her "rosas de otoño".

At to the play itself, the plot is interesting, enlivened by clever dramatic situations; the outcome is logical; the sinners are punished; and the repentant husband Félix is allowed to return to the sanctity of his home and his long-suffering wife. All this is naturally and capably handled. It is true that, as in the previous plays studied, the author resorts to melodramatic effects and excessive sentimentality: the sick child, whose very breathing is described by Enriqueta in a maudlin manner; and the too sudden conversion of Félix. All these seem overdone.

The characters are not very realistic. Mercedes is Eguílaz's idea of the ideal wife, and an ideal is just what she turns out to be. She is not real. Her plight is what many women must content themselves with, but her attitude seems abnormally idealized. She is always waiting gratefully for her husband, is loving in his care, devotes all her time to him and to their child, sells her diamonds to set up a trust fund for the *niño*, then gives her husband the money for him to gamble away, without a murmur of dissent. She never reproaches him for anything. Like so many of the "good" characters in these thesis plays, Mercedes is too perfect. She is drawn all out of proportion in order for the playwright to cite her as an example of "la mujer casada". Viewing the other woman from the opposite extreme, we demur at believing Enriqueta is an oft-found Spanish wife. Félix and Manuel suffer from the same faulty character-delineation.

Though the *moraleja* is clearly brought out in the course of the play, Eguílaz, to make sure his ideas on the distaff side of matrimony were readily comprehensible, makes Mercedes the "raisonneur", particularly in her conversations with Enriqueta, who —being a *mujer cursi*, the exact opposite of Mercedes— serves as a foil for her.

In addition to Eguílaz's proposal of Mercedes as the Spanish wife of the year 1861, he may be trying to praise Spanish womanhood as idealized in Mercedes, the woman who will remain loyal and true in the face of such trials as those forced upon her by her husband, who seems to have a mistress, complains of his solicitous wife, and will gamble with her money, callously unconcerned for the health of his only son.

In resumé, it can be added only that Eguílaz was as socially concerned as Tamayo, but far shallower. His plays make no pretense to lofty philosophy; they state no problems and solve none; they will disturb no one's conscience nor will they excite any very deep emotions. The sentiments they arouse are measured by the range between a smile and tears. But the moral observation underlying each is just, and often the working out of this truth is ingenious; and if the decent folk whom the author is addressing do not leave the theater in a state of emotional bewilderment, at least they have not been bored, and incidentally they may have been led to search their hearts a bit and profit by some lessons. They have not wasted their evening.

Aside from the vitality of the *zarzuela* it may be said that the most significant feature of the theater after 1850 for the development of the modern Spanish drama was the thesis play of Tamayo y Baus and López de Ayala, the Spanish counterpart of the dramatic tendency manifest in the plays of Augier and Dumas *fils* in France.

Tamayo's *La bola de nieve* (1856), which attacks jealousy and is reminiscent in its theme of *Un hombre de mundo*, may be said to initiate the problem play into the Spanish theater. *Lo positivo* (1862) is an attack on materialism, and *Lances de honor* (1863) deals with the dueling question and solves it in accordance with orthodox Catholic views.

Ayala continues the tendency in *El tejado de vidrio* (1857), a new treatment of the Don Juan theme; in *El tanto por ciento*

(1861), which attacks the money craze and resultant evils; and in *El nuevo don Juan* (1863), which attacks once more the eternal fatuous type symbolized by the protagonist.

The thesis drama of the period, however, is hardly more than a continuation of the high comedy exemplified in Vega's *Hombre de mundo,* which in turn is a continuation of the Moratinian comedy. To be sure, the national traditions of the *Siglo de Oro* merge with this current—especially in the neo-calderonianism of the early dramas of Ayala. But, while the point of departure in the work of Tamayo and Ayala is the thesis, their theses are the moral, or social-moral theses of the type inherent in the plays of the Moratinian tradition. The chief distinction is that the theses of Tamayo and Ayala are emphasized more than the moral themes of the Moratín plays and their continuations; but the thesis is still primarily moral, like the Moratinian theme, rather than social as in Augier and Dumas *fils*. Furthermore, the thesis has not yet reached the point, in the Spanish plays, where it is taken up and discussed pro and con in the manner of argumentation and debate. Though emphasized, the emphasis upon it does not throw it out of harmonious proportion with other elements of the play.

CHAPTER IV

ROMANTICISM IN REALISM

The monarch of the Spanish Stage in the last quarter of the nineteenth century was José Echegaray (1832-1916), the first Spaniard to receive the Nobel prize for literature. Echegaray was a university professor of mathematics, engineer, statesman, and playwright who did not care how hard he pushed his plots or worked his characters. The result was a new sort of Romantic melodrama, emphasizing passion and leaving out minor considerations such as the Middle Ages, local color, and other appurtenances of earlier Romanticism. Echegaray's scenes and characters are usually contemporary and apparently realistic. It is their volcanic passions and problems that now seem to us exaggerated, and give an impression of artificiality. [1]

The first of these Echegaray plays to be examined here is *O locura o santidad*, a three-act drama in prose, presented at the Teatro Español on January 22, 1877. The play is dedicated to Antonio Vico. The scene is Madrid.

Lorenzo Avendaño, a wealthy business man, has a daughter Inés, whom Eduardo, a duke, wants to marry; they are much in love. Juana, a former servant of Lorenzo's family, is brought to his home extremely ill. She tells him that she is his mother, that she had been imprisoned years before, having been accused of stealing a medallion worn by the woman thought to be his mother. Honest Lorenzo informs Eduardo's mother that he, Lorenzo, is not an Avendaño, hence must call off the marriage of Inés and

---

[1] ADAMS, N. B., *The Heritage of Spain*, New York, 1943, page 242.

Eduardo; and he plans to give his fortune to its rightful owners. Juana, sorry for having caused this misfortune, just before she dies, denies what she had told Lorenzo, and consequently the whole group fears that Lorenzo is losing his mind. He claims, nevertheless, that he has proof (a letter which Juana has given him) of his strange story. But Juana has removed the letter replacing it with a blank piece of paper. A doctor Bermúdez and two attendants from the *manicomio* present themselves, and Lorenzo, aware that they believe him mad, says, "I'll go quietly."

Echegaray's thesis is that real honesty may be mistaken for madness. In order for him to prove this thesis he had to imagine an unusual set of incidents — not impossible at all, but certainly a rare coincidence of events. As for the presentation of the thesis, Echegaray very skillfully combined plot and thesis, achieving success not usually enjoyed by the writer of thesis plays. Dramatic interest is maintained throughout, the mistaken idea that Lorenzo is mad being impressed inexorably upon his friends; and we are ever conscious of the tragedy of his action and the consequences on Inés. Therefore, this thesis play is also a really great tragedy.

One of the best or most significant points to be observed in *O locura o santidad* is that the thesis is presented entirely through the relentless action of the play. Echegaray's ideas are not forced upon the audience. He does not need a *raisonneur* to help him explain his purpose in writing the play. In this particular of dramatic technique, we can see the Ibsen influence ever so apparent in Echegaray's plays. Primarily the play was written to entertain, and entertain it does; and the thesis is always subordinated to the plot.

As to the characters, there is really only one, Lorenzo, and he is magnificent. There is majesty in this creation. The others are not unusual, but neither are they ordinary. Most admirable is the fact that not one of the minor characters is out of proportion to point up the thesis. All are normal human beings, acting in a human way. Only the situation is unusual. For this romantic situation Echegaray has created a romantic hero. Though Echegaray appeals often to the "nerve ends", rather than to the mind, *O locura o santidad* remains an absorbing thesis play, a rare combination of dramatic interest and effective presentation of the thesis.

Typical of Echegaray's thesis plays is *Lo que no puede decirse*. This three-act drama in prose was first presented in the Teatro Español, October 14, 1877. The scene is Madrid.

Federico and quick-tempered Gabriel are supposedly sons of Eulalia and Jaime, but it is revealed that Federico is really the illegitimate son of Eulalia and a Sir Arthur Brandley, who had raped her twenty-four years before. Patrick, an Englishman with whom Jaime does business, recognizes Federico as Arthur Brandley's son and gives the boy the bequest left him by his father, some thirty thousand pounds. Eulalia and Jaime, who knows the story, agree to give the money to Federico but determine to try to keep the news of its coming a secret from their sons. It leaks out; scurrilous attacks appear in the newspaper; and Gabriel feels some explanation is necessary. Whence the money? Finally Eulalia tells him in a letter the whole unpleasant story, and she drinks poison, her secret out, the irreparable damage done.

The thesis is that, because of the curiosity, moral prejudices, and usual misunderstanding of people in some situations, the truth cannot be told, lest the telling occasion tragic consequences. As Jaime says of the mob, "Lo sabe todo... y no saben la verdad". And Echegaray effectively proves his thesis, though the circumstances imagined as background for it are often rare. The purpose of keeping secret the tragic history of Federico's birth is understandable, and such action would be considered normal anywhere. But the Spanish idea of honor is at stake here, and Echegaray's solution is typically Spanish. It the outraged husband did not kill his wife, she was expected to commit suicide, according to the literary or dramatic code. The dramatic conflict inherent in this situation is overwhelming.

As he had done with *O locura o santidad*, Echegaray presented his thesis entirely within the dramatic action of the play. It is always in evidence and running its inevitable course to a tragic conclusion. The author did not have to employ the *raisonneur* to present his thesis.

The play generally conceded to be Echegaray's best is *El gran Galeoto*. This drama in three acts, in verse, was first presented in the Teatro Español, March 19, 1881. The scene is Madrid.

A curious and novel prose prologue opens the play. It begins with a dialogue between the would-be playwright Ernesto, the protagonist, and his benefactor Julián, with whom he lives. Ernesto reveals his eagerness to write a play different from anything ever written: no love interest, *todo el mundo* to appear, the play to begin at the end; and there are other strange devices which he plans to use to write this play of plays. Teodora, Julián's wife, much younger than he, enters to tell us that many people (*todo el mundo*) have inquired about Ernesto. When they leave, Ernesto sits down to write his drama, *El gran Galeoto,* calling on Paolo and Francesca da Rimini to help him, recalling the beautiful story of Dante's meeting with Francesca in the fifth canto of the *Inferno,* whence, as we shall see, the title, the "Great Go-between".

Ernesto does not have a job; he lives as a guest in Julián's house because Ernesto's father had helped Julián get started in business, and Julián feels great responsibility toward the family. The young Ernesto realizes that he is imposing on their hospitality, but is persuaded to remain. Neighbors and relatives are beginning to gossip, suggesting that Teodora and Ernesto, who until now have something like a brother-sister relationship, are in love. On hearing this careless gossip, Ernesto voices Echegaray's thesis:

> "...lo que dice la gente,
> con maldad o sin maldad,
> según aquél que lo inspira
> comienza siendo mentira
> y acaba siendo verdad."
> Act I, Scene II

To preserve his self-respect Ernesto accepts Julián's offer of a position as secretary. Julián's suspicions are aroused by his brother Severo's suggestions that Ernesto and Teodora are in love.

In Act Two, Ernesto has moved to a modest room where he continues writing. A copy of Dante's *Divina Commedia* lies open to the episode of Paolo and Francesca. Ernesto is planning to go to Buenos Aires to make a living. Julián and Severo come to try to dissuade him. Ernesto is not at home. Pepito, Severo's son, reveals that Ernesto is to fight a duel in defense of Teodora's good name. This comes about naturally, but it is not his prerogative to defend another man's wife. So Julián goes to find out where the duel will be fought. Ernesto returns to his room. Teodora comes to advise Ernesto of the impropriety of his dueling, and both are unaware that the duel is going on at that moment elsewhere. While she is in Ernesto's room, Severo enters, bringing Julián who has been wounded in the duel, which he had fought as his responsibility. Teodora is thus surprised in Ernesto's room.

Act Three takes place in Julián's home where he lies mortally wounded and convinced of Teodora's infidelity. Mercedes browbeats Teodora to try to make her confess her "guilt". Ernesto returns to Julián's house, takes them all to task; Severo orders Teodora to leave; Ernesto makes him apologize to her; Julián dies; then Ernesto tells them that he will take Teodora away with him.

"Lo quiso el mundo. Yo su fallo acepto."

Echegaray's thesis, as stated by Ernesto is Act One, is that it is possible for a mistaken idea to be repeated often enough, through carelessness and malice, to produce the situation suggested. Or, that malicious gossip may throw an innocent girl into the arms of the innocent man with whom she has been accused of wrongdoing. This rather far-fetched thesis [2] is artfully assisted in its development by the author's competent use of the charming legend of Paolo and Francesca in respect to the idea of the "go-between" or intermediary, which brought Ernesto and Teodora together, namely, gossip, "el gran Galeoto". Galeoto is the Spanish equivalent of the French Gallehaut, the intermediary who brought Lancelot and Guinevere together. Paolo and Francesca had no such go-between; the book they were reading was their guide to love.

It appears that it was Echegaray's high ambition to make neither a comedy of gossip, like *Le Misanthrope*, nor a tragedy of slander, like *Othello*, but a unique play midway between — a tragedy of idle, non-malicious gossip, the only achievement of its kind in dramatic literature.

As to his handling of the thesis, if we accept the rather unusual character of it, Echegaray was eminently successful in its develop-

---

[2] Unfortunately, Echegaray weakens his statement in the lines that follow. He is unwilling to take a definite stand.

ment up to the final disposition of the two chief characters. The author convincingly introduces the characters and events or situations in almost every case until that in which Teodora, left alone, unsheltered, about to be cast out of her own house by Severo (representing the harsh, unrealistic, incorrect attitude of society toward a suspect though wholly innocent woman), is rescued by Ernesto. Is this real? Would she have gone away with him? At the beginning of the play the author definitely establishes that Teodora and Julián are happily married. There is nothing in the entire play which would lead the audience to believe any illicit affair was in progress. Therefore, we can hardly believe that Teodora loves Ernesto or that his generous act of rescue is prompted by anything other than generosity. It seems that with circumstances as they are, her husband dead, the ignominy, the vituperation heaped upon her by Severo and Mercedes and the snide Pepito, were she completely innocent in her own mind, Teodora would not want to lend credence to the general belief that she was guilty by consenting to go away with Ernesto. Yet, she may have realized that if she was to be driven out, she had no other recourse. Ernesto was her only hope. In this way Echegaray seems to prove his thesis, but it remains somewhat strained, and the outcome seems not the result of their mutual love, but rather desire for support on Teodora's part.

The characters are generally welldrawn and realistic, not overemphasized for presentation of the thesis. The situations are such that normal people would react to them as Echegaray would have them do in *El gran Galeoto*. But Teodora's visit to Ernesto's room is a serious error, because it completely destroys her character. No respectable woman would have done this, yet we know Teodora is respectable. On this rash act the resolution of the play depends. With such rapid action as there is in this play, and the plot made interesting through compelling character-creation and spectacular scenes, Echegaray did not include a *raisonneur* in *El gran Galeoto*.

This play is world drama. The ideas therein embodied are universal and apply to all peoples and to all epochs of human history. We are face to face with the great and ugly monster, slander, at all times one of the greatest evils of society. Echegaray has treated this social problem with originality and some success, and the results of calumny are painted so black that the lesson given to the public is unforgettable.

Among the really representative plays by Echegaray, *Conflicto entre dos deberes* is perhaps the most typical. This drama, in three acts and in verse, was first presented in the Teatro Español, December 14, 1882. The setting is Joaquín's house in Barcelona.

Amparo and Raimundo, a young lawyer, are in love, ready to be married, but Raimundo seems to prefer waiting until he is better off financially. He has her father's permission to marry. A Dolores de Medina seeks legal advice from Raimundo (she had heard about him because she and Amparo were schoolmates). Dolores seeks redress for the theft of a million pesos stolen from her murdered father seven years before. She has a letter which gives proof of the identity of his murderer. It is Joaquín, of course, who claims he killed in self-defense. So Raimundo is now involved in a conflict between two duties. Prudencio, Raimundo's self-seeking uncle, slyly suggests that Amparo steal the papers from Raimundo, fearing that Raimundo will somehow be prevented from supporting him. Baltasar, Amparo's brother, wild and headstrong, threatens bodily harm to Raimundo if he does not soon settle the case, and Raimundo seems to waver in favor of Joaquín and Amparo, but he remains true to the law. Raimundo promises Joaquín to save him from death. Baltasar rushes in, demands the papers, wildly asks Joaquín if he is the murderer; he replies in the affirmative, is challenged to a duel which Raimundo fights in his stead. Raimundo and Baltasar return later, the latter mortally wounded. Joaquín is so upset at this turn of events, that he kills himself. To conclude the tragedy, Amparo curses Raimundo and leaves him.

It is curious that Echegaray should entitle a play with the very phrase which might characterize many of his works. As Hurtado y González Palencia say: "El móvil de sus dramas es con gran frecuencia la duda material o moral." The thesis here is that it is of little moral value to fulfill a duty or obligation if, in so doing, one loses his own happiness and destroys that of others. Raimundo is caught, trapped, between two forces, two moral obligations, and the conflict is a terrible one, inevitable tragedy the only outcome possible. Raimundo is much like Lorenzo in *O locura o santidad*, assuming gigantic proportions. The play becomes comparable to the Greek tragedies in scope and significance, and in this thesis play we find Echegaray reverting to his earlier manner of writing, like that of *La esposa del vengador, Correr en pos de un ideal, En el seno de la muerte,* and *La muerte en los labios,* recalling the romantic plays of the 1830's, their antecedents. The majority of these plays are essentially romantic. Love, truth, and honor are at stake in all of them, the predominant idea a conflict between duties. The author has made the punishment of sin his moral code, and in the above romantic plays, most of them composed in verse, he often presents very emotional scenes even to the point of sacrificing the form for the substance. Sin and its consequences are set forth in the blackest colors so that the public will hate it.

Echegaray is an old-fashioned moralizer. He is so relentless in punishing the guilty that in his plays the innocent are often punished as well. He is a keen observer, understands human passions, and continues in the Spanish drama many of the old ideas of *pundonor*, but in the presentation of his eternal conflicts between duties he often exaggerates, and some of his plays are artificial and overdrawn as human documents. His figures are titanic, even sublime, but often they are grotesque and too good or too bad for real life.

In *Conflicto entre dos deberes*, however, Echegaray's characters are realistic. We must sympathize with Raimundo because he really has a problem, fortunately not one which must be faced too often. Incidents leading up to the conflict in this drama are cleverly prepared and executed, and are basically acceptable. But coincidences occur, and a great deal depends on chance. As is frequently the case, in a melodramatic production of this kind *vraisemblance* has to suffer in deference to the "coups de théatre". The familiar ideas of honor and vengeance are employed to advantage in this play, and it is a compelling tragedy; it was written for people who liked to be shocked, who appreciated mighty scenes of emotion, and who did not want their minds too much disturbed by profound thought or philosophy.

Conflicto entre dos deberes is not one of the author's great plays, but it deserves attention as an interesting thesis play. The characters are realistic, and, though the situation is rare, the development of it is normal, logical, and capably handled.

As is generally known, toward the end of Echegaray's second period of playwriting he fell under the influence of Henrik Ibsen, the Norwegian dramatist. The play which shows more Ibsen influence than any other by Echegaray is *El hijo de don Juan*. This drama in three acts and in prose (as were most of his later works) was first presented in the Teatro Español March 29, 1892. The author in "dos palabras a manera de prólogo" declares that it was inspired by reading Ibsen's *Ghosts*.

The scene is a mansion, a *sala-despacho,* and the time the early 1890's. Don Juan has been married to Dolores over twenty-five years, but he still relishes his gay and rather loose premarital scrapes. It is through descriptions and reminiscences of some of these that his character is revealed; he is hardly remorseful. His son Lázaro, an artist, is betrothed to Carmen, the daughter of Timoteo, Juan's old friend and crony. It is discovered that due to Juan's profligacy Lázaro's brain is diseased, and he is losing his mind. So, he cannot marry Carmen. The play is in essence simply this.

Though the plot can be summarized in so few words, *El hijo de don Juan* is powerful drama, a magnificent play. The pathetic situation, sad, bitter, heart-rending, leading to the inevitable tragic ending leaves the reader exhausted and overwhelmed. The thesis is a revision of the biblical warning that the sins of the fathers shall be visited on the children, even to the third and fourth generations. And, in these moving scenes, Echegaray preaches an unforgettable lesson against unbridled license. One of the most striking aspects of Echegaray's dramatic technique as exemplified in *El hijo de don Juan* is the carefully executed, inexorable, onrushing force of the drama, from the description of don Juan's wicked life, the first suggestion that all is not well with Lázaro, the introduction of the pathetic figure of Carmen (the most victimized of all who suffer as a result of Juan's evil ways), their betrothal, the visit of the doctor Bermúdez who advises against the marriage, the brilliant conclusion to the second act, the suggestion at the beginning of Act Three that Lázaro's health may be improving, the gentle, moving scene between Carmen and Lázaro longing for the ceremony to be performed, the tragic irony of the penultimate scene in which Lázaro's mind begins to fail, the forced separation of Lázaro and Carmen, lest the mad man harm her, and then Lázaro's departure into madness.

This is excellent drama, brought off without a hitch. The thesis is presented wholly in the dramatic course of the play. No *raisonneur* is necessary. *El hijo de don Juan* could have been an effective instrument against vice and its sometimes fatal consequences. Many a man in the audience witnessing this play must have experienced some uncomfortable moments in recalling recent visits to the *templa amoris*.

The parents of Lázaro, don Juan and Dolores, are interestingly, competently, and realistically delineated, he the profligate father, she the too indulgent mother, both of whom worship their only son, all of which enhances the tragic impact of his loss.

In conclusion, Echegaray treats several problems in these five plays. His thesis is that real honesty may be mistaken for madness in *O locura o santidad*. *Lo que no puede decirse* is an attack on prejudice, the thesis being that because of the curiosity, moral prejudices and usual misunderstanding of people in some situations, the truth cannot be told, lest the telling occasion tragic consequences. *El gran Galeoto* is an attack on slander or gossip (with or without malice), the thesis being that a lie told often enough can produce the real thing. In *Conflicto entre dos deberes*, Echegaray tries to point out that real duty ought not be carried to extremes, that is, to the point of destroying people or their happiness. And the last of these plays, *El hijo de don Juan*, purports to show that the sins of the father are often visited with tragic consequences upon the children.

In all of these plays Echegaray makes a plea for the improvement, not necessarily of Spain alone, but of all mankind. His theses are sometimes far-fetched, portraying the kind of situation or incident which would be rare and unusual and unlikely to occur. But his dramatic technique is so great that with all these initial circumstances he is usually successful in developing a gripping play containing a sound moral lesson.

CHAPTER V

MINOR PLAYWRIGHTS

Nineteenth-century Spain had the most prolific period in all of her long history in this genre. Thousands of plays, good and bad, were written to entertain and to teach. Though there were bright stars in Spain's galaxy of playwrights, in some cases they shine the brighter in comparison with several good dramatists whose fame was not so widespread. Notable among these was Rodríguez Rubí (1817-1890), who contributed almost a hundred dramatic works of various kinds to the vast collection.

Of his "comedias de costumbres contemporáneas" there are four of "moralidad indirecta", as Hurtado y González Palencia call them: *El gran filón, Fiarse del porvenir, El arte de hacer fortuna,* and *La flor de la maravilla. Fiarse del porvenir* is a slight moral lesson on the dangers of improvidence and the advantages of preparing for the future. *La flor de la maravilla* is little more than a piece of the moment, of no significance now, but at the time of its presentation it was generally believed to contain political satire.

The two remaining *comedias,* however, are a picture of the times, each reflecting the author's earnest desire to call attention to the sorry state of Spanish society in the second and third quarter of the century. Rodríguez Rubí's dramatic production was extensive, spread over almost four decades. One of the earliest of his works, *El arte de hacer fortuna,* a four-act *comedia* in verse, was first presented in 1845. This play is political satire, not mordant, caustic, violent, or advocating revolution, but rather a play written to entertain, a comedy of manners, yet clearly of "intención política".

The play is not short, though the plot can be summarized in a few words. With the help of Facundo, Angel —an unknown amateur politician— attains considerable success at the expense of a marquis who had assisted Facundo in his own rise on the political ladder, showing that personal obligations are to be disregarded when one's own political ambitions are at stake.

In two characters the author contrasts the types of men who appear in politics. One, Facundo, is the proverbial political type who is brash, bold, self-advancing by any and all means, interested only in himself. Service to his constituency and to his country seem to him of no importance. Angel is the other, elected to office as *diputado*, wondering how he, unworthy as he feels himself to be, could have been elected, though fervently desiring to be of the best service to his country. The title is justified in that the play is concerned mainly with Angel's rise to fame and fortune through the political machinations of the wily Facundo.

All this is really secondary to the author's primary purpose in writing an entertaining comedy. The emphasis, thus, is on the entertainment features, not on a thesis. It is a play of indirect moralizing which has been mentioned as characteristic of Rodrígez Rubí's works. A light political satire, it deftly points out how so much of man's advancement depends on chance, and that it is sometimes just as easy for a person of little ability to attain a position of importance as it is for a highly trained and intelligent person to do. Curiously enough, however, the author seems to have failed in the first purpose and attained but little success with his second. The play itself is confused and not often entertaining, though the politico-moral purpose is apparent and readily assimilated.

The last of Rubí's successful works was *El gran filón*, a *comedia* in three acts, in verse. It was first presented in the Teatro Español in November, 1874. In the dedication to Ramón Campoamor y Campo-Osorio, Rodríguez Rubí deplores the conditions prevailing in Spain at that time (1870's). He quotes journalists of the day to support his comments, emphasizing the need and obligation of everyone's help. The author says, "Yo acudo con mi escaso contingente por si en algo puedo contribuir a sofocar el incendio de la patria... He procurado exponer con la debida mesura algunos de los vicios sociales más arraigados ya en nuestras costumbres".

Jacinto assists all his friends, in the humble boarding house where he lives, with money obtained by blackmailing a general Adán and his wife, each of whom had been involved in clandestine love affairs. Through his information about these two he establishes his friends in responsible positions. Jacinto has such a hold over the general that, though Adán is the chief deputy in Congress, Jacinto tells him what to do. Jacinto — opportunist that he is, changes sides and supports Adán's rival, Valentín, who not only beats him in an election (with Jacinto's help), but also plans to take his daughter away with him.

As will be observed, there is little plot to this play, perhaps too hastily written on a sudden whim suggested by the words of the unique title. "El gran filón" means the "great lode" or "vein" from which great wealth may be mined. So, by extension, in this case, it means the blackmail with which Jacinto not only becomes rich but also makes his friends wealthy as well. The play, like *El arte de hacer fortuna*, has a confused plot structure, the characters are strained beyond belief, none of them seems real flesh-and-blood, and there are few good scenes to recommend this play. The moral lesson is vague. It is difficult to determine just what it is. It seems to be that Adán's past and that of his wife have caught up with them, and thus he deserves to be defeated in the election. Yet in this way the promoter-blackmailer Jacinto goes unpunished, and the moral lesson is misleading. The whole plot seems preposterous. Hence, as Hurtado y González Palencia say, "En las comedias de costumbres contemporáneas Rubí llevó a escena muchas veces cuadros políticos, con tendencia satírica, a veces exagerados hasta lo grotesco, v. gr., *El gran filón*, el último de sus éxitos, de la que dijo acertadamente un crítico que era como una mujer que en el conjunto resultara agradable, y en cuanto a los detalles se le notasen algunas imperfecciones".

Despite his apparent weaknesses in this field, Rubí was still a popular playwright, in his day "lord of the comic stage", and in some of his best works he appears as a progenitor of modern comedy based upon a more realistic study of society. He was in this respect an innovator, like Ventura de la Vega, and aided in the transition from Romanticism to the drama of Eguílaz, Ayala, and Echegaray. [1]

Almost contemporary with Rubí, being only slightly younger, was José Marco y Sanchís (1830-1895). Not so prolific as Rubí, but continuing the tradition, Marco cultivated the "comedias de costumbres". Among his works "de tendencia moralizador" are *Libertad en la cadena, La feria de las mujeres,* and *Las esculturas de cera.*

Libertad en la cadena, a *comedia* in three acts, in verse, was first presented in the Teatro del Príncipe, June 13, 1857.

Ernesto and Julia are about to be married. Carlos and Matilde, friends of the former, are *novios.* Carlos is a bachelor who refuses to give up his freedom. All work to have him marry. In Act II Carlos calls on Ernesto and Julia and learns that their marriage is not always perfectly happy, though Ernesto dutifully defends his state, because Julia is petulant, won't allow him to "go out with the boys". Ernesto, not to be ordered about, goes out anyhow, and Julia admits to her friend Angustias that she cannot stand his being away, will do anything to have him want to remain with her. Ernesto returns, they make up, and all is forgiven. Carlos, however, is not convinced that he himself will find "libertad en la cadena".

This is a summary of the very slight plot, simply a series of highly amusing comic scenes, in which the author suggests the thesis that a married man has more freedom than a single one, and that a man should marry early. Showing what a man might suffer during a long engagement, this play is a realistic reflection of the character of the *noviazgo* in Spain, and the play would perhaps be understood and accepted best by a Spanish audience. The play is a light treatment of an interesting subject. There is enough of the serious to give it some impact, and it is therefore a cogent plea for matrimony. With *Libertad en la cadena,* Marco has given to the Spanish theater a charming little play, amusing yet stating a thesis. There is something of Bretón de los Herreros in Marco in this benign picture of nineteenth-century society.

---

[1] MÉRIMÉE AND MORLEY, *History of Spanish Literature,* New York, 1930, page 484.

One of Marco's most successful plays first presented "con extraordinario aplauso" in the Teatro del Circo, December 2, 1871, was *La feria de las mujeres*, a *comedia* in three acts, in verse.

Three sisters —Amelia, Aurora, and Concha— have come to a resort near Valencia for a vacation. Amelia and Aurora are eager to find a husband. Concha, really the most marriageable of the three, does not seem overanxious about it, going about her daily household chores goodhumoredly and dutifully. This resort is a "feria de las mujeres", i.e., a place where women go to meet prospective husbands. Two men, Luis and Ernesto, have rented a house next door, and soon become interested in the girls. Amelia and Aurora pale in comparison with the wifely charms of Concha, and Ernesto wins her promise of marriage, Luis not wanting either of the two remaining.

The thesis, quite secondary to the all-important purpose of entertainment, is clear and artfully presented: that the home-loving, capable woman is to be preferred to the *dama cursi*. The thesis is supported by the author's moralistic advice offered to the frivolous, vain, empty-headed woman who desires a husband. To point out his moral lesson, Marco believed a *raisonneur* necessary, and not just one, but two — Ernesto and Prudencio, the latter the girls' father.

There is a good example of Marco's comic talent occasioned by a high wall separating the back yards of the two summer houses. Over this wall several engaging scenes are enacted, not really important to the plot, but usually quite amusing.

Another in the series of *comedias* which Marco wrote as a picture of Spanish society in the 1870's was *Figuras de cera*, a *comedia* in three acts, in verse, first presented in the Teatro de la Comedia, January 18, 1876. On the page preceding the "Personajes" the author quotes a passage from Sor Inés de la Cruz:

"Hombres necios que acusáis
a la mujer, sin razón
sin ver que sois la ocasión
de lo mismo que culpáis;
¿para qué os espantáis
de la culpa que tenéis?

>   Queredlas cual las hacéis,
>   Hacedlas cual las buscáis."

From this passage Marco makes his play.

Benito is too harsh with his daughter Elisa, who is about to marry Julio. Her father wants her to be a stay-at-home, a drudge, almost a servant, believing that such is a woman's duty. Julio, on the other hand, wants her to be more careful in her dress and appearance, to learn to play the piano and to become a lady of fashion. In Act III they have been married for some time, and Elisa has followed completely Julio's prescription and even exceeded his hopes. She is loud, flashy, never cares for the house. Julio regrets this, of course, but is unable to do anything about it. It is of his own doing.

With the two unusual characters Benito and Julio, extremes in their ways, inclinations, and ideas about their womenfolk, Marco has constructed a comedy with several entertaining scenes. The play teaches a moral lesson too — again dealing with the problem of education of women, but with a different treatment. The moral lesson, as the quotation shows, is that women are made (become) to the taste of those who love them (fathers and husbands). It depends then on the tastes of the creator what the woman will be: *mala o modelo*. Benito and Julio both were in the wrong. Benito attempted to rear Elisa as a servant, seeming to have little regard for women. Julio made her "demasiado señora".

Though the moral lesson is readily assimilated, there is a *raisonneur* —Antonio— Julio's father. He has many things to say on the subject of education of young girls for wives. The characters Benito and Julio seem warped the better for the author to teach his lesson. The shock experienced by the audience at the sight of the changed Elisa in Act III might occasion laughter rather than dismay. *Figuras de cera* is a comedy throughout, but it contains a thesis, which is frequently obtrusive, and the two are not harmoniously combined.

Echegaray started a school. Among those who to some extent followed his lead Eugenio Sellés (1844-1926) deserves a prominent place. His first great success was *El nudo gordiano*, a drama in three acts, in verse, first presented in the Teatro de Apolo, November 28, 1878.

Carlos discovers that his wife Julia has a lover Enrique, his business associate. To protect his honor Carlos declares that he himself has been guilty of infidelity, and for this reason his wife has requested separate maintenance. Thus he justifies in secret his determination to put her away. In Act II Julia hears from her daughter María that some woman is being talked about scandalously, and Julia realizes that it is she herself, now living apart from Carlos, who does not believe in divorce. Carlos and Enrique have reached the dueling point at the end of Act II. Julia has been locked up in Carlos's house. Carlos is slightly wounded in his duel with Enrique. Julia begs for a divorce, Carlos refuses, and she leaves. Not content with this, he runs after her, and —offstage— he kills her, thus preserving his honor.

This is the ironic solution to the play which is a bitter attack on the tradition of no divorce in Spain. In Carlos's house everyone is miserable. Yet nothing can be done. As Fernando, Julia's brother says in Act Three:

> Así son las cosas. Pacto
> con Dios o con el infierno,
> en el bien como en el mal
> el matrimonio es perpetuo.

This is a serious play, unlike the light treatment given various social conditions by Marco y Sanchís, for example. In *El nudo gordiano,* an apt title indeed, the author has described one of the saddest of conditions, a condition still prevailing in Spain in the mid-twentieth century. Here is a woman clearly guilty of adultery, who must go on living with a man whom she no longer loves, and he, of course, does not love her. What is worse is that their young (15) impressionable daughter María has to live in these unfortunate surroundings, when the situation could be remedied simply by divorcing Julia. But Carlos is the personification of the church and the strong hold it has on the minds of the Spanish people; traditional stubborn Catholic heritage keeps this family in torment. So terrible is the force of Julia's sin, however, and so strongly does it affect Carlos's sense of honor that he commits murder to right this wrong, adding greater tragedy to the already tragic situation.

There is no warping of characters here to present this thesis play. The character of Carlos is brilliantly done, while the others are well above average. Though no *raisonneur* seemed necessary, discussion takes place about the problem among the important characters, discussion presented naturally and unobtrusively, listing various hardships which can be overcome by divorce. Sellés delivers an eloquent argument for divorce in *El nudo gordiano*.

Another Sellés play "docente y de tesis" was *El cielo o el suelo*. This three-act drama in verse was first presented in the Teatro Español in January 1860.

Pablo has grown up in a monastery and is so much a Christian that he plans to give all his worldly goods to the poor. He loves Luisa, the sister of Rafael, his business associate. She is promised to Eduardo, however. Rafael plans to seduce Blanca, Pablo's younger sister. When this is a *fait accompli*, Christian Pablo astonishes Rafael by saying "Yo perdono". But Rafael provokes a duel, throwing several banknotes in his face, as if thus paying for Blanca's services. This is too much to bear, and Pablo forsakes *cielo* for *suelo*, fights and kills Rafael. This means, of course, he cannot marry Luisa, though he is exonerated by law from the murder of Rafael. One of the minor characters, Andrés, makes the author's sad commentary on the situation: "La sociedad —no te asombre— es así."

The similarity of this play and *La locura o santidad* (1877) is at once apparent, though in *Cielo o el suelo* the insanity idea is but once and only slightly suggested. Lorenzo's honesty is Pablo's Christianity. The play itself, though in many points stark melodrama, is quite worthwhile. The conflict is absorbing, though incidents seem forced at times, leading up to Pablo's decision to be a man and defend his sister's honor, *suelo* overcoming *cielo*, a dramatic conclusion. Yet the dénouement seems weak and inconclusive. In short, it is confused and too diffuse to give the lesson the impact a better playwright might have done. Pablo is a perfect characterization, somewhat overdrawn for emphasis, but in this lies Sellés's weakness. Pablo is too good to be true, giving away his money and refusing at first to defend Blanca.

Actually Pablo is an interesting portrait of a human trying to be Christian, having the customs of society thrust upon him, and having to accept them because the laws prescribe it, even though in his conscience they seem to go against the tenets of Christianity. Indeed the customs of Spanish society made Pablo a murderer in his own eyes (we must remember that Pablo grew up in a monastery), and —though this is an extreme case— it is a real indictment of Spanish society itself. Hence we have a thesis here, an attack against many things: duelling, *pundonor*, and what they lead to — their consequences. It is not specific, not as direct, as Tamayo's *Lances de honor*, yet a general thesis is clearly evident. The tone is really not that of Echegaray's plays, yet Sellés is certainly influenced by him. The play is romantic, melodramatic, and even has a final touching tableau.

Still showing his fondness for startlingly symbolic titles, Sellés presented *Las esculturas de carne*, a three-act drama in verse, at the Teatro de Apolo, February 1, 1883. Apathetic, lethargic Benigno is the father of Miguel, young, ambitious, forward-looking, idealistic. He loves Emilia, daughter of Clemente, who is the exact counterpart of Benigno. Don Juan hopes to marry Emilia, but is trying also to seduce Carmen, Benigno's young wife. Miguel suspects Juan's duplicity. In Act II, the whole group resides in a summer chalet at Biarritz. Juan is revealed as the persistent lover his name implies, and Miguel warns Emilia against him. She seems to want to marry Juan, but Clemente will not give his consent. Juan goes to Paris with Carmen, who seems completely amoral. Miguel sees all this, but Benigno and Clemente refuse to wake up to their duties. In Act III Juan and Emilia have married, but he is still interested in Carmen. Miguel, still loving Emilia, resents Juan's treatment of her, and extremely honor-conscious, beats him to death offstage. Thus everyone loses, and the audience is taught a moral lesson.

The thesis is that people should assume their responsibilities and do their duty, lest by their own apathy, excessive tolerance and unconcern, they lose all. The title is effectively symbolic, because these aptly named individuals Benigno and Clemente are not men. They are only "statues in flesh". The author effectively proves that the unconcern of Clemente and Benigno provoked their own undoing in the tragedy which wrecked the lives of six people.

Again the author sets up one giant of a man, *un santo* or *tonto*, as he is variously called, opposed to all the rest of the characters. He is too good, too honorable, too impulsive to be real. His passion for honor makes him appear foolish. Yet his actions are always above reproach, except maybe for a little unpremeditated eavesdropping in which he learns of Juan's and Clemente's duplicity. Carmen actually admits she has been wicked and when trying to get out of the situation is dragged in deeper and to her own sorrow by the libertine Juan. The lesson is taught through the natural development of the plot and through the preaching of Miguel.

The play depends much on chance, overheard conversations, the usual devices. Sellés does not reveal unusual originality. Benigno and Clemente are warped beyond recognition as men to emphasize their lack of character. Such people do not exist. Great attention to detail in staging reveals much Echegaray influence on Sellés, as well as his attempt to create in Miguel the giant of Lorenzo in *O locura o santidad*.

The last in the series of Sellés's plays to be considered here is *La vida pública*. This *comedia* in four acts, in prose, was first presented in the Teatro de la Comedia March 6, 1885. Apparently it failed because in a note to the reader the author declares that "el fracaso de mi comedia es merecido y justo". In this he admits the weaknesses of the play, but defends "su valor de realidad". He adds that he "intenta demostrar una tesis".

Happily married Patricio living with his family in a small town of Andalucía is urged to run for *diputado* in Madrid. He accedes to his friends' wishes against his and his father's (Modesto) judgment, wins the election, and moves to Madrid, only after mortgaging his property in order to make the move. His wife and son Julio have social ambitions. As Patricio had expected, their troubles were soon magnified: duel-threatenings, his daughter's reputation suspect as a result of his rapid advancement, hangers-on, sycophants, job-filling, featherbedding; and his daughter Sofía breaks up with Prudencio, her long-time *novio*. To save his family he sends them all back to Andalucía, he having to remain in Madrid as *ministro*, having given so much to his public life that his family life no longer exists.

In this homely effort Sellés essays a plea *pro domo sua*. The thesis seems in opposition to those of his other plays in which he advocates civic responsibility and participation, but the obverse of the coin the author believed just as fertile material for his dramatic talents. And he does state a good case against such total devotion and dedication to politics that one's family is neglected or even sacrificed for the advancement of the individual.

Sellés wrote other plays with a thesis element, but the absence of good characterization makes them generally ineffective, and most of the topics under discussion in them are not applicable to modern society.

Likewise continuing the Echegaray traditions was Leopoldo Cano y Masas (1844-1904). Three of his better-known plays are *La opinión pública, La pasionaria,* and *Trata de blancos.*

The first of these, a drama in three acts, in verse, was given *estreno* in the Teatro de Apolo, October 17, 1878.

Matilde as a young girl was seduced and deserted. Her illegitimate son she gave (fearing public opinion) to a woman, to be cared for. All this is unknown to her rich husband Juan by whom she has a fifteen-year-old daughter, Gloria, who has a weak heart. Gloria loves Juan's secretary Luis, who is at best an opportunist in his financial dealings. Not interested in Gloria, he seems rather too much interested in Matilde. A man, hoping to take advantage of Matilde's fear of public opinion, comes to her seeking money (blackmail) telling her that his mother was the woman who had reared her son, giving her a picture of him which her son had sent to his foster mother; of course it is Luis. This situation at the end of Act One is what public opinion caused. The situation is made more acute by current gossip (public opinion) that Luis and Gloria are lovers. She and Luis have been seen coming from a humble house together, where, unknown to public opinion, they have been engaged in social work. All this makes public opinion demand that they must marry, an impossible thing. The effect is heightened by Juan's surprising Gloria in Luis's arms—in the dark. Luis had thought she was Matilde. Gloria in the confusion had fainted. At this point Ketty, the English wife Luis had deserted, appears, declaring she is his wife (thus removing the suggested incest possibility). Luis, a despicable character, informs on Juan to the police in order to have him arrested so he can run away with Matilde. She still has not told him of their relationship. Luis enters, threatens to kill her if she won't run away with him. She says "Then kill your mother!" In argument over possession of the pistol Matilde's lips approach Luis's head just as Gloria enters the room. This is too much for her weak heart. Misunderstanding, she dies. Luis goes offstage where he shoots himself. Matilde falls to her knees crying "¡Jesús! ¡La expiación!" Angel and Virtudes, gossips who have helped to provoke this tragedy, rush in to offer their assistance to Matilde. Public opinion demands it.

La opinión pública is a complicated, highly involved play, the plot of which depends largely on chance, mistaken identities, letters, photographs, and one or two good dramatic situations. It is not characterized by originality. So improbable are certain actions that they seem ridiculous. The play is very weak. There is not an admirable character in it. The characters are confused and not clearly delineated in any case. There are some strikingly emotional scenes, but their development and presentation seem faulty, amateurish, incomplete.

The thesis, that public opinion is responsible for the tragic events which transpire in this play, is far-fetched and unlikely. Yet its power is inescapable in the play, as it is in real life. It seems almost a character of the *dramatis personae*. The author has to resort to almost every melodramatic device known to accomplish his purpose and maintain interest. As real drama the play is not outstanding. It appeals rather to the emotions than to the mind. There are too many characters, and in the opening scenes so much exposition takes place that it is difficult to bear in mind all necessary details. Two interpolated parables lengthen an already overlong play. The Echegaray influence is great. Similar to Echegaray's technique is Cano's use of Romantic ideas: Luis as the long-lost son with the taint of illegitimacy and the impossible love theme between Luis and Gloria, which harks back to Greek tragedy. The unity of time is observed, the action lasting from seven p. m. to five a. m.

As to the thesis, the lesson is clear from the start, and it is presented in the action of the play; the words "opinión pública" are frequently expressed to give the reason for certain actions. No *raisonneur* appears. In his character development Cano has greater success with the women than in his description of the men.

Generally thought to be Cano's best play is *La pasionaria*, a three-act drama in verse, first presented in the Teatro de la Zarzuela December 14, 1883.

Angelina, who loves Marcial (now in Cuba), is about to marry Justo, a man thought wealthy, to save her father Perfecto in financial straits. Justo is a despicable character, cowardly and dishonest, who had seduced Petra, a poor girl, who comes with her daughter Margarita to see him. Petra is the illegitimate daughter of Perfecto. Marcial returns from Cuba and is recognized by Petra as her one-time protector, and he promises to stand by her, threatening bodily harm to Justo if he refuses to give Margarita his *apellido*. Justo has influence with a judge who is about to remand Petra to a charity hospital and Marcial to an asylum for the insane. All except Marcial share the same opinion of Petra as a fallen woman. Even Margarita's love seems won away from her by Angelina. Marcial tells Justo he plans to marry Petra to restore her reputation. But an uncle has bequeathed Margarita a fortune which Justo wants. He forces Petra to sign a document (which gives him the right to Margarita's money) threatening that she will never see her daughter again otherwise. Perfecto enters, sees Justo mistreating Petra, and seizing Justo's knife stabs him to death. Marcial tells the judge that the "delincuente es la iniquidad de la ley" which condemns irrevocably the woman who has been seduced.

La pasionaria, like *La opinión pública*, is a long involved play with too many characters, too many details. The presentation of events and the motivation are confused. The passionate scenes seem insincere. There is not one good character either in the author's delineation or in the moral fiber of the individual. All are diffuse. Even the brave giant Marcial (Echegaray influence?) is described as a *duelista* and *ateo*. And he is the *raisonneur*, preaching against the vicious law which protects the adulterous man. The thesis is that the world should not condemn the woman (and pardon the man) who sins for love but once, but rather should consider the circumstances which accompanied the act. The author attacks this *ley inicua* which prevails today and has always prevailed in "civilized" society.

The thesis is valid, and the play makes the need of change apparent and urgent. But the play itself is not a great piece of drama. It is a long, drawn-out melodrama. Questions raised are not clearly resolved. Perfecto is left unpunished, possibly to give emphasis to the iniquity of the law which denounces the fallen woman in society. As is usually the case, the thesis is effectively presented at the expense of the play. *La pasionaria* is much too long. Indeed, many verses are marked with a note from the publisher to indicate that they were omitted in the presentation of the play. More could have been left out. The characterization of Angelina is obscure. Is she good or is she one of the company of Lucrecia, Perfecto's greedy sister, Justo, and Perfecto? Perfecto is really a nonentity in the piece, as is Lucrecia too. Neither contributes much to the action of the play.

Typical of Cano's plays deploring the evils of society in the latter part of the nineteenth century is *Trata de blancos,* a three-act drama in verse, first presented in the Teatro Español, February 10, 1887.

Modesto and his sister Tula are trying to get his daughter Luisa well married. She is interested in doing social work, has accumulated much money for certain Spanish colonizers in South America who are suffering privations. A certain César de Madrid, promoter and racketeer is exploiting these colonizers for his profit, and all of Luisa's relatives and friends pay him blackmail. To escape payment, all are trying to have Luisa marry him. Modesto appropriates Luisa's money to pay off César. Only a young newspaper columnist whom Luisa loves, namely Juan de Dios, determines to resist this scoundrel. Juan is named heir to a large sum of money, but because his ancestry is uncertain, if he accepts the money, his personal reputation is at stake. It could mean ruin. César is about to foreclose on everyone, and to save them, Luisa says she will marry him. In Act III they have just been married. Juan returns to see Luisa, finds César, his machinations exposed by Juan, about to flee to South America. César is about to shoot him when the judge who had reared Juan (really César's illegitimate son) from childhood, enters through a window, shoots and kills César.

This hodgepodge of situations carelessly and ineptly thrown together was intended to be a play. It resulted, however, as poor melodrama. The plot is so complicated and so involved, so many actions are unmotivated that relationships of the various characters are confused beyond understanding. It is difficult to determine what the conflict is, even to take sides. It is a *mélange* of individuals, each of whom has an evil character (except for Luisa and Juan), the author's portrayal of the worst of Madrid society.

All profited from César's crookedness, yet only César was punished—and that inadequately and melodramatically done, and in a most unlikely manner, when the judge arrives in the nick of time in the last scene of the drama.

All the characters are money-mad and it is in connection with these financial dealings that the double-meaning title is brought into the picture: "Dealing in coins or money" (a "blanco" is a small Spanish coin) and "dealing in white (people), hence slaves" —as almost all of the disreputable characters in this play are. They are as much César's slaves as are his worker-colonists in the New World. It is a revealing and a disgusting picture of society, of course much overdrawn, the characters resulting mere puppets who never attain the dignity of individuals. The wicked are too wicked. The good are angelic, otherworldly, completely unreal. *Trata de blancos* is not really a thesis play but purports to be social drama in its attack on the crooked politicians, "caciques", who assume great powers because of the apathy, disinterest, and excessive tolerance of most people. Juan, the *raisonneur*, assists the author in his moral lesson with frequent allusions to conditions, criticism of local politics, innuendoes against *diputados* in their immunity (and abuse of it) from punishment. In this respect Cano is a progressive, anticipating the practice of later *dramaturgos* who create a *raisonneur* who is young, progressive and forward-looking as opposed to the former custom of having an older man as *raisonneur* wanting to return to the "good old days".

The usual criticisms of too many characters, too much forced action, long speeches, little character-development, too many asides—all apply in *Trata de blancos*. This play is not entertaining, and as social drama it is not effective, because of the confused presentation of the author's attack.

Another and perhaps greater playwright of the last half of the nineteenth century was Enrique Gaspar (1842-1902). Of his total dramatic production approximately one fourth is in the field of the social drama. The plays included in this category are: *Las circunstancias, La levita, Don Ramón y el señor Ramón, El estómago, La lengua, Lola, Las personas decentes, La huelga de hijos,* and *La eterna cuestión.* They were written during the years 1867-1895, and are eloquent witnesses to the fact that Gaspar was struggling unabatedly to win a place for the drama of social criticism in the minds of the theater-going public.

The influence of a changing environment upon the character of a well-meaning but weak-willed individual is the theme of *Las circunstancias,* a three-act *comedia* in prose first presented in the Teatro del Príncipe, November 18, 1867.

Miguel is a weak-willed individual who is influenced by his immoral dishonest wife Elvira to take advantage of *circunstancias,* opportunities to better their financial and social position. Through certain circumstances a large sum of money belonging to María, daughter of his friend Antonio, falls into his hands, and Elvira urges him to appropriate it to his own use. Ironically, the banknotes which he steals are counterfeit, and Miguel is arrested. This is too much for him, and his moral collapse is complete; he bitterly regrets his surrender to fortuitous circumstances.

The play is striking in its clarity and simplicity. Gaspar has subordinated everything to the demonstration of his thesis. The plot, situations, and dialogue are built around the central theme of two characters who, at first in moral conflict with each other, are later united in their attempt to make the most of chance. They are ordinary individuals, normal and lifelike. They are stamped with none of the freakish and violent qualities which Echegaray gave to those of his characters who were subjected to moral crises. They do not appear to be monsters of crime, and the realism of the play consists precisely in the fact that they are not represented as such. No fantasy or poetical scenes suited Gaspar. It was his avowed purpose throughout his career to send his audiences home shivering from a contact with social problems even closer than that afforded by reality.

No traditional *raisonneur* appears in *Las circunstancias.* The lesson is taught through the logical and natural development of the action. Yet Elvira and Miguel act as their own *raisonneurs.* They comment upon their own behavior and regard themselves psychologically. They are sufficiently intelligent to understand their own motives, even though understanding does not give them mastery over their selfish impulses, and there is no need of a third person in the play to explain these motives philosophically to the audience.

Yet in spite of these worthwhile attributes of dramaturgy, the critics were not kind to Gaspar. He represented too much of a change from established practice in the social theater. He was too real for their tastes. During the period in which Gaspar wrote, the Spanish bourgeoisie was in the process of consolidating its social position, and so found it necessary to erect formal standards from which it was disgraceful to deviate. People who received a certain education were so satisfied with their cultural level that they felt it incumbent upon themselves to maintain a style of living which would afford a dignified setting for their attainments. When economic disaster visited the members of this class, they avoided the shame of a deteriorated external appearance by recourse to whatever ingenious devices would conceal their precarious status from the eyes of the world, and they made heroic efforts to remain in possession of social deference. Gaspar's next drama is a satirical attack on this stupid middle-class vanity, which he symbolizes by a characteristic garment worn by those entitled to the rights and privileges of this group. The *levita*, or frock coat, was the robe of honor of those who were but one step removed from the sweaty proletariat. With his frock coat on his back, the middle-class Spaniard felt strong, warm, and secure, even though his stomach might be empty.

In *La levita*, a three-act drama in prose, first presented in the Teatro del Príncipe, February 29, 1868, Gaspar rips its glossy fabric to pieces. His ridicule and irony join hands in an effort to demonstrate the immorality of venerating an object which was so often kept in good condition only by the destruction of conscience.

Cesáreo and Emilia have known better times but are now quite poor, though they strive to maintain appearances symbolized by the *levita*. Valeriano, a rich shopkeeper who rose from the proletariat, loves their daughter Isabel and wants to marry her. When Cesáreo loses his job he and Emilia believe it best for their own interest that Isabel marry Valeriano, who is uncouth but honest, and she is beginning to admire him. An acquaintance, Manuel, visits them, stays long, and abuses their hospitality; and

Cesáreo even steals some money to maintain the "front" of comfortable respectability. Valeriano discovers Manuel to be a swindler, and the two come to blows over a receipt. In the scuffle, the pocket of Manuel's *levita* is torn. Appalled at the implications of this coincidence, Cesáreo decides to live in the future in accordance with the dictates of his conscience. Abandoning hypocrisy, he confesses his true situation.

Gaspar succeeds admirably in this play in conveying the desired philosophical and social effect. The drama has a force that could not fail to move the spectators. The greater part of its power may be attributed to the selection of so novel a scapegoat as an article of clothing, to symbolize the hopes, fears, ambitions, and the tragedy of a particular class of society. Many persons doubtlessly saw themselves in the stage characters, and must have been frightened or annoyed at the reprimand Gaspar was giving them.

The critics of the rose-colored-glasses school were again displeased by the depiction of unpleasant truths upon the stage. This hard, dry, cutting exposé of human wickedness was contrary to the accepted principles of dramatic art, which was supposed to devote itself entirely to the entertainment of the customers, noble people of altruistic sentiments, with insipid intrigues of love. Yet it seems that in his dénouement Gaspar was to a certain extent compromising with public taste. At the moment when moral disaster is about to overwhelm him, Cesáreo reforms, and we have a happy ending. It is more than likely that those citizens who had reached a stage of degradation equivalent to Cesáreo's were not saved; but Gaspar, having made his point, was willing to allow his audience its accustomed sigh of relief at the conclusion of the drama.

Though Cesáreo and Emilia are excellent characterizations, real human beings whose plight arouses sympathy, the figure of Valeriano is not equally convincing. He is too good, too self-sufficient, and too stable to be lifelike. In his sudden leaps from the unlettered shopkeeper to utter socio-philosophic thoughts appropriate only to a person of an extensive cultural background, Valeriano frequently becomes Gaspar expounding his thesis. Valeriano then is the *raisonneur*. Isabel is devoid of personality, too sweet, gladly immolating herself for her parents' sake. Manuel is well depicted; in him Cesáreo is permitted to observe a picture of himself as he will be in a few years unless he repudiates his foolish vanity.

Gaspar was a typical nineteenth-century dramatist in his penchant for the theatrical, and in his anxiety to enhance the interest of his plays, at least those of his early period, by creating startling effects calculated to pull the spectators straight up in their seats. Although he never failed to present living characters whose collective actions impressed some lesson of social ethics upon the public mind, he was not above introducing stage tricks which amuse the audience and testify to the author's ingenuity. Gaspar's French contemporaries, Dumas *fils* and Sardou, prided themselves on such intermittent shocks of excitement: their influence on Gaspar in this respect must have been considerable.

One of Gaspar's most important plays of social significance was *La lengua,* a three-act *comedia* in prose, first presented in the Teatro de Apolo, April 8, 1882. Devoid of much of the philosophical reflection which is an integral part of the preceding dramas, *La lengua* is light in tone and pointed in meaning.

Julia soon after marriage finds her husband Enrique in company with his former mistress, whereupon she leaves him to earn her own living. After six years of separation Enrique begs to be taken back. Successful in the theater, she refuses, thinking he wishes to offer her money. Julia's friends are determined to convince one another that she is carrying on an affair with Terencio, who, flattered, does nothing to give the lie to these whisperings. Enrique comes to believe what he hears. And Julia refuses to offer any explanation which will clear her. His wife's dignity dissolves Enrique's suspicions, and they seem reconciled.

The *raisonneur* is Don Antero, a physician, though his socio-medical commentaries are superfluous. The potential evil of gossip is defeated by the valor and self-sufficiency of its target. That is the thesis of *La lengua.* As will be noted, just a year before the appearance of this play, written in China where Gaspar was in the consular service, Echegaray's play on the same theme of gossip, *El gran Galeoto,* had its *estreno.* But these two plays have nothing in common. *El gran Galeoto* is written in sonorous verse that was a delight to capacity audiences, while *La lengua* is in prose, a fluent and literary, though unacademic dialogue which is a perfect reflection of the characters who employ it. *El gran Ga-*

leoto is a tragedy; the protagonists of the play are powerless to combat the insidious murmurs which bring catastrophe in the death of Don Julián and the unpremeditated liaison of Ernesto and Teodora. Echegaray does not endow his characters with will strong enough to save them from their invisible enemy. *La lengua* is a comedy-drama. Julia is a match for gossip; she believes that those whose consciences are clear should turn deaf ears to what others say about them, even though personal happiness may be sacrificed. One's self-respect and sense of integrity will more than compensate for the loss of those worldly pleasures which may be retained only by temporizing with the viciousness of people's tongues. By holding to her principles, she succeeds in retaining her husband and her own self-esteem, and in administering a crushing blow to malevolence. The figure of Julia is an innovation; she is the first modern woman to appear in the Spanish theater. Indeed all the characterizations are realistic and carefully delineated in *La lengua*.

Of Gaspar's last four plays of social criticism, three, namely, *Lola, La huelga de hijos,* and *La eterna cuestión,* are concerned with the intimate problems of marriage. Gaspar wrote many thesis plays (at least eleven) but it is impractical to try to discuss them all in detail here. For this reason only the last one, dealing with the problem of adultery, will be considered.

La eterna cuestión, an *esbozo dramático* in three acts, in prose, was first presented in the Teatro de la Comedia, December 10, 1895.

The conflict centers about the adulterous relationship between María and Enrique. When the play begins, this state of affairs has presumably existed over an extended period of time, without the knowledge of Carlos, María's husband, who considers Enrique an intimate friend of the family. María jealously flares forth when she learns that Enrique has fought a duel to protect the honor of another woman. He tells her he must leave Spain on business, and she does not believe him, unable to face the prospect of having lost his love to another woman, yet she does not feel any responsibility toward her husband for her own adultery and treachery to Carlos. María is transfixed with horror and self-condemnation when she learns from Carlos that Enrique is in love with her daughter, Amparo. María is possessed by two overpowering emotions, her jealousy as an abandoned mistress and her overwhelming grief as a mother who has ruined her daughter's opportunity for happiness. Amparo overhears a conversation between María and Enrique and learns her mother's secret. María begs Carlos to kill her and implores pardon of her daughter, but is repulsed. Carlos indicates that this is her punishment.

Thus Gaspar concluded his crusading career as a dramatist as he had begun it, shocking the native audiences by his unadorned realism and his frank and necessarily brutal presentation of a social problem. *La eterna cuestión* was too much for the squeamish public, and for most of its backward and sentimental moral advisers, the critics. It was not that adultery had been unheard of in the theater before Gaspar's preoccupation with this theme in his last drama, for it had furnished the motive for many plays which were wildly applauded by the spectators, in direct proportion, however, to the fantastic melodrama, and unrealistic manner of its presentation. Audiences had thoroughly enjoyed the denunciation of adultery in resonant, impassioned verses, with vengeance inflicted upon the culprits by husbands swollen with *pundonor*, and had risen happily from their seats when the guilty persons had expiated their sins by death. By no stretch of the imagination could the spectators connect what they had seen on the stage with life outside the theater.

Gaspar forced the playgoers to make this connection between art and life, and they protested. The matter-of-fact tone of *La eterna cuestión* terrified them; the tragedy was unbearable because credible. They felt that such a tragedy might enter the lives of their friends, or their own. The actors spoke the language of the contemporary environment, and behaved in general in a manner appropriate to actual human beings. The final horror was the absence of vengeance, which utterly annihilated whatever feelings of complacency still remained to the moral mind of the Spaniard. The curtain descended upon a tragedy that was beginning, not upon one which had been brought to a conclusion in the last scene.

In *La eterna cuestión* Gaspar fulfilled his intention of showing the unromantic and repulsive side of adultery. Although the actual situation which he pictures is not by any means a general one, the lesson loses none of its force or plausibility. Many were the virtuous cries of moral indignation raised at Gaspar's lifelike depiction of the consequences of adultery.

Gaspar wrote, as mentioned above, other thesis plays: on education—*Don Ramón y el señor Ramón;* a curious play entitled *El estómago,* the thesis of which is that human beings are the victims of their struggle for physical survival, that their moral constitutions and actions, both for good and evil, are determined by their psychological state; *Lola,* a plea to married men and women who have separated because of incompatibility of character to reconsider their decision, to reflect on the harm they have caused their children by destroying their family life, and to endeavor to patch up their differences. *Las personas decentes,* presented January 31, 1890, the only play of Gaspar's to be received with unqualified applause by both press and public, showing his gifts as a satirist and as an observer of society to the greatest advantage, a fierce satirical indictment of the greed, selfishness, and corruption rampant among the members of the middle class of Gaspar's time; and *La huelga de hijos,* a virulent attack on the conventional Spanish standards of feminine behavior and morality. Gaspar was ahead of his time. Had Spanish society chosen to adopt the reforms suggested by Enrique Gaspar in his provocative thesis plays and dramas of social customs, its present state would be much improved. A sincere crusader, he was misunderstood and unappreciated. His dramatic works deserved better treatment than they received.

Although Gaspar Núñez de Arce is best known for some volumes of verse, *Gritos del combate, Versos perdidos, Poemas cortos,* and is generally regarded as one of the leading poets of the late nineteenth century, he wrote also three plays variously called "alta comedia" and, by him, in an *advertencia* to a volume in which they appear, "drama íntimo, de la conciencia", "comedia de costumbres", and "drama de tendencias sociales". Two of these belong to the field of social drama, *Deudas de la honra* and *Justicia providencial.*

Deudas de la honra, a three-act drama in verse, was first presented in the Teatro Lope de Vega, January 17, 1863.

Ana, the daughter of don Andrés, has been seduced by Felipe, by whom she has had a child. Felipe seems to have deserted her. Juan, a friend of Andrés and Ana, leaves town to be with his dying mother. And Felipe returns, suspecting Juan's interest in Ana. Indeed, when Ana at last confesses her sin to Andrés, he suspects Juan as the father. Andrés had declared that in his youth he had seduced a number of women, and that when seduction occurred it was the woman's responsibility. When Andrés learns that Felipe was the seducer, he prepares pistols for a duel if Felipe won't marry Ana. Juan announces that on her deathbed his mother declared Andrés was his father, whereupon Andrés says he will recognize him as his son. Juan refuses the generosity preferring that the scandal not be made public. Andrés feels that his own seduction of Juan's mother has been avenged by the seduction of his daughter by Felipe. Felipe refuses to marry Ana and refuses to fight Andrés, but accepts a challenge from Juan. Felipe still refuses to marry Ana, suggesting that he will later. Citing scripture, Juan persuades Andrés to forgive Ana and to accept the child. Felipe who has overheard all this, enters to say he will marry Ana.

The plot is far-fetched and unlikely. The extreme case of the moral problem gave Núñez considerable trouble in developing the plot in a logical manner. Motivation is bad, revealing the author's inexperience as a playwright — this was his first dramatic work of any importance. Coincidence and chance produce much of the action. The notable feature of this play is the presence of highly dramatic and touching scenes. Though not very good drama, in its shock effect it was appealing perhaps to some women in the audience.

Juan is the *raisonneur,* largely responsible for bringing about a happy ending to this *drama íntimo.* His moralizing could very well apply to similar cases which would be likely to occur in double-standard Spain. The other characters are convincing but not outstanding creations. Though hardly a thesis play, *Deudas de la honra* advocates greater understanding in cases of this kind where the woman, though at fault, deserves consideration. In many respects it has all the earmarks of a typical Echegarayan drama, though antedating by ten years Echegaray's earliest.

The second of Núñez's social dramas, *Justicia providencial,* a three-act drama in verse, was first presented in the Teatro Español, November 24, 1868. In an *advertencia* to an edition of his works Núñez made the following comments on this play:

"*Justicia providencial...* drama de tendencias sociales, en que se tocan algunos problemas que el movimiento intelectual y la lucha de los intereses plantea incesantemente en nuestros tiempos, y en que apunta, porque el carácter sintético del teatro no consiente mayor desenvolvimiento, la influencia que en el seno de la familia y en el orden de los afectos pueden producir determinadas corrientes de ideas."

Having studied seven years in France Juan returns to the house of his aged guardian Antero, who has a young wife Irene. Fernando, an old friend of Juan's, saying he wants to be near Juan, takes the house next door to try to seduce Irene. Santiago, Fernando's father, comes to spend the night, bringing a bag of gold which he has collected from a debtor. Perico, Antero's servant, having read Renan and other French materialists, determines to steal the money, planning to fasten the blame on Fernando, who intends with Perico's help to visit Irene that night. In the confused scene that follows, it appears that Juan is the thief, and Fernando, unsuccessful in his seduction attempts, escapes identification. Irene suspects Perico, however, whose conscience makes him tell Juan what has happened and so help to prove Juan's innocence. Fernando returns the next day, and to keep her husband from killing Fernando, Irene hides Fernando in a closet with an iron door; Antero realizes at last why Fernando is around all the time. Antero in a melodramatic whim, ignorant of the fact that Fernando is in the closet, locks the door declaring that he wants no one ever to enter the room which has concealed such base villainy.

The play is an improvement over Núñez's earlier dramatic efforts, but this one is unnecessarily complicated. All of the characters represent a step forward in Núñez's attempts at characterization. Perico and Juan stand out as being the most original characters that have appeared in the two dramas examined.

The author's moralizing tendency finds expression in his attack upon the evil influence of French materialists upon the youth of Spain. In scene 12 of Act II, Antero's speech serves as the author's thesis. He declares that visionary youth is seeking liberty and progress by rebelling against authority and following godless doctrines. Yet he optimistically feels that youth will eventually realize the evil effects of atheism and will return then to a belief in God.

Thus Núñez de Arce seems a proponent of the school of Tamayo and Ayala in his concern for social customs. As Hurtado and González Palencia say, Núñez's works are "de realismo urbano y moralizador, al modo de las de Ayala". He is for progress, but seeks improvement in social conditions by restoring respect in established traditions. He is a conservative, not the radical who was to appear in later nineteenth-century playwriting.

But in his dramatic technique he fails to rise above the level of mediocrity. He has difficulties in his involved complicated plot construction. Some characters are interesting and sympathetic, but none is truly lifelike, the good too good, the evil characters overdrawn for emphasis on the moral lesson. Moral preaching is not excessive, although the author's didactic aims naturally detract from the artistic worth of these plays.

CHAPTER VI

DICENTA AND GALDÓS

Toward the end of the nineteenth century some playwrights concerned themselves to a certain extent with the ideas of progress and the resultant improvement of Spain and the lot of the Spanish people. Though there had been and were at the same time many others so inclined, Joaquín Dicenta (1862-1917) and Benito Pérez Galdós (1843-1920) indicated more than a passing interest in social drama as a means for achieving social progress. Both men were not only interested in fame and glory to be found in writing successful plays, but as evidence of their serious concern for the state of Spanish society, they belonged to progressive political liberal and socialist parties and participated openly in their programs for reform. Dicenta and Galdós began writing for the stage at about the same time (1888-1892). But as Dicenta's plays were the first to appear, it seems advisable to begin with them before taking up the study of those of Galdós, which actually reflect more of the modern touch.

"Joaquín Dicenta, siguiendo, en parte, la escuela de Echegaray, fue el primero que escribió dramas de asunto social tendencioso." [1] There had been, to be sure, other playwrights with similar interests, but it was Dicenta who first openly courted trouble with established customs and authority. Dicenta's chief claim to fame is his interest, then, in the lowest economic groups. Of him it is usually said that he brought the proletariat to the stage, not for

---

[1] HURTADO Y GONZÁLEZ PALENCIA, *Historia de la Literatura Española*, Madrid, 1943, page 997.

picturesqueness or for comic relief as in the *siglo de oro* drama, but as protagonist. Some of his work is highly romantic. In fact, Dicenta has been called "a Romantic in a workman's blouse". His dialogue is the natural speech of the proletarians he represents, and he makes no attempt at prettiness or elegance. He certainly enlarged the scope of the Spanish stage.

Los irresponsables was the first of Dicenta's social dramas to appear. This three-act drama in verse was presented in the Teatro Español, November 27, 1890.

Felipe, a newcomer to the small village where this play takes place, is seriously in love with Margarita, beloved only daughter of don Anselmo, a wealthy farmer. Carlos, a *madrileño* cousin of Margarita's, comes to pay court to her, recognizes Felipe, learns he is already married, and tells this to Anselmo. Anselmo throws Felipe out after telling Margarita his secret. She soon learns why Felipe cannot ever marry her: that, though his wife is profligate, the law does not sanction divorce. So Margarita goes to see him. He asks her to go away with him: their only hope to be together. She cannot do this and hurt her father. Irate Anselmo rushes in to take her home. Felipe declares death his only recourse. Still in love with Felipe she runs to him. Anselmo shoots at him as Margarita leaps between them. She is killed — the tragedy is complete.

In this play Dicenta makes a strong case for adequate divorce laws in Spain, using the case of an unfaithful wife and her husband's not being allowed legally to divorce her (separation being the only alternative open to couples who cannot continue living together, neither party to marry while the other lives). The background material for this prime motivating factor is clearly expressed and yet not overemphasized. The terrible position in which it places Felipe is effectively presented in Margarita's sincere description of the sudden development and consummation of their love before the action of the play begins. She does not feel remorse for her act believing their love will be crowned in marriage. The conscience factor thus laid upon Felipe makes for potentially good drama. He is obsessed with the disturbing factor of his loss of honor in his wife's continuing adultery with various men, in addition to his responsibility toward Margarita.

A point to be made in Dicenta's favor is that he convincingly brings in these factors and conclusively resolves them all in the short course of the play.

In presenting Dicenta's ideas on progress, Felipe seems to stand out, as did Pepe Rey in Galdós's play *Doña Perfecta*. Felipe calls progress "la más justa de las leyes" —saying this while lamenting the absence of divorce laws in Spain.

It has been said that Dicenta is a member of the Echegaray school, and in the characterization of Felipe his influence is more than apparent. In addition to being overdrawn, this individual has most of the characteristics of the Romantic hero; of unknown (at least to Anselmo's group) ancestry and origin, slightly eccentric —this to prepare the reader for the surprising news of his marriage— and in love, an ill-fated love. What is more like Echegaray is the astonishing *coup de théatre* in the final scene when the tragedy is made complete with the sacrifice of Margarita in the accidental shooting by her father.

With regard to the author's purpose in advocating divorce laws, such procedure was certain to meet with opposition, especially from the church, and in fact the Teatro Español itself must have felt the pressure, for, according to Mérimée and Morley in their *History of Spanish Literature, Los irresponsables* "caused some scandal" there. This play must have been pretty shocking to the conservative bourgeoisie present in the theater. Yet it must have awakened a gleam of hope in the minds of the more enlightened members of the audience, and especially those who found at the time the bonds of matrimony somewhat restrictive. In connection with this facet of Dicenta's play, Padre Andrés, Anselmo's friend and adviser, is presented most sympathetically. He is not the Inocencio of Galdós's *Doña Perfecta,* nor the fiend in priests' clothing conjured up in later revolutionary writers in the days of the second republic (1931-1936). So the play is only slightly slanted in favor of progress. It was early yet, only 1890.

Also reminiscent of Echegaray is the "conflict between two duties" which might have beset Carlos, who, after promising to reveal nothing of Felipe's unwise relation of his unfortunate marital experience, immediately forgets his vow and tells all to Anselmo. His action is certainly well-motivated. He did not feel obligated to Felipe, whereas he hoped to marry Margarita. He had everything to gain and nothing to lose in this revelation. His jealousy alone (he had been roundly rejected by Margarita) could have prompted his determination to enlighten Anselmo and Margarita.

The weak spot in the drama is Felipe's completely unmotivated disclosure of the facts of his life; how he had surprised his wife in another man's arms and had killed him, but that his wife had escaped to continue her adultery promiscuously, and that he had to leave Madrid to avoid the scandal to settle in the village to try to escape the ignominy. It is not explained why he did not kill his wife later. The coincidence of Carlos, who recognized him, coming to the village is satisfactorily explained. But Felipe had no reason to give him this information. Of course, subsequent action depends on Carlos's possession of this information, but he might have learned it differently and more logically.

It is curious to note here that this play is written in the traditional verse form. We shall see that his later plays, and all his serious plays after this one were written in prose, some of it the language of the people, unadorned and very real. Indeed, in the early scenes of *Los irresponsables* Dicenta's description of the landscape waxes quite lyrical, charming, and attractive, but it advances the play very little.

The play for which Joaquín Dicenta is best known in Spain and abroad is *Juan José*. This three-act drama in prose was first presented in the Teatro de la Comedia, October 29, 1895. A drama of the proletariat, its setting is the *barrios bajos* of Madrid.

Juan José is a poor laborer in love with and living with Rosa, who, though an opportunist, for the moment, at least, is in love with Juan José. Isidra, an older and more experienced woman, advises Rosa to forsake Juan José for Paco, the foreman of the factory and thus assure herself a better living. When Juan José and many others are laid off at the factory, life seems grim for them, and Rosa resents it so much, that, to assuage her suffering, José tries to steal for her, is caught and sentenced to prison for eight years. In Act Three Juan José has served eight months in the Cárcel Modelo. His friend Andrés writes him what he feared to hear: that Rosa is living with Paco. No longer concerned for his honor or life, Juan José escapes, surprises Paco as he is about to enter Rosa's apartment and, giving Paco an opportunity to defend himself, kills him. Rosa screams for help, and, though not intending to do so, in the confusion, Juan José strangles her.

Frankly revolutionary social drama, *Juan José* purports to show the miserable condition of the laborer in Spain in the last decade of the nineteenth century, and symbolically points out the only way of effecting a change: by uprising and overthrowing the ruling classes. This policy seems indicated, in the opening tavern scene, in a halting perusal of a revolutionary newspaper by a poorly schooled friend of Juan José. In the discussion which followed among the *bebedores,* the symbolism is evident that the chief male characters, Juan José and Paco, represent respectively the downtrodden proletariat working at two to four reales a day vs. the high living, big spending higher classes. Paco himself, not of the aristocracy but an overseer who has forgotten his own origin, having risen to a position of power, naturally allies himself with the group that feeds him.

Juan José is good drama for several reasons. The plot is simple but real and intensely dramatic, essentially unadorned, except for the Echegaray influenced *coup de théatre* in the offstage murder of Paco and the onstage accidental death of Rosa in the last act. The killing of Paco is regarded among critics as unfair and cowardly. But in the disclosure of his murder of Rosa immediately —only seconds— afterward, he declares he gave Paco a chance to defend himself. The reader has already been told in graphic terms of Juan José's predisposition to violence. Unless Paco was portrayed onstage as quite a big bully, then his death might appear an act of cowardice on the part of Juan José. The author undoubtedly felt that this detail was effectively explained in Juan José's declaration and let it go at that.

The protagonists's protagonist, Juan José himself, is what the author is sometimes called: a "romántico en blusa". Rosa is his first love, and he loves her deeply, disregarding her apparent instinct for self-preservation which prompts her easy morals and willingness to seek a better situation. In this factor lies the essential tragedy of the drama: Juan José will make any sacrifice for Rosa while she, though seeming to love him, and she later declares that she did love him, is too willing to go to live with another man when Juan José is jailed for attempting theft for her sake. The author handles this skillfully and dramatically. Until the last scenes the spectator entertains the hope that they may be reconciled, but when Rosa shows her feelings for her present lover Paco, her real character is at last made clear. And, ironically enough, though Juan José came to her apartment to kill Paco, he did not intend to kill her. Her own selfish disposition provoked her death. And she died, still loved by the romantic Juan José. Reminiscent of the Romantic plays is his final observation, effective, yet highly melodramatic, and thus guaranteed, as Echegaray had done, to please the more *sensible* of his audience: "¡HUIR!... ¿Y pa qué voy a huir?... ¿Qué libro con huir?... ¡La vida! ¡Mi vida era esto (por Rosa), y lo he matao!"

As will be noted in the spelling, the author was trying to portray the proletariat speech in his social drama, thus adapting effectively the atmosphere of the lower classes to the stage. He was so seriously concerned that its use be understood that he wrote a note about it at the beginning of the play: "Cuiden los actores que representen esta obra, de dar a los personajes su verdadero carácter; son obreros, no chulos, y, por consiguiente, su lenguaje no ha de tener entonación chulesca de ninguna clase." *Juan José* is no parody, no humorous portrayal of the illiterate. Dicenta employs the speech of the unlettered to describe them as they are and to plead for assistance, for attention, for salvation, so mean was their lot.

In keeping with the setting of life in the *barrios bajos* is Dicenta's depiction of the *mores* of the people. Toñuela and Andrés, good friends of Juan José's live together openly, known to all that they are unmarried. Likewise do Juan José and Rosa. The tone of the piece therefore is sordid, realistic, even in this respect reflecting what there was of the Zola influence on Spanish authors of the period, and especially on Dicenta. There is no attempt at explanation of this detail. It is accepted and understood. Its moral implications do not enter into the significance of the play.

Also in accord with the speech of the lower classes, and with Dicenta's preoccupation with them is his use of prose in *Juan José* a better play than *Los irresponsables* and a more modern appearing piece than the work of his predecessor and mentor, Echegaray. The effect could not have been so striking or so realistic, had Dicenta resorted to the resonant verse of his antecedents in Spanish drama.

Isidra (la "señá" Isidra) is an important personage in *Juan José* although she does not often appear, because it is she who persuades Rosa to desert Juan José for Paco. In this, and in receiving payment for her efforts, she is the modern counterpart of the "go-between" of the *Libro de buen amor*, Trotaconventos. But she is sadly lacking in any of the prototype's winning qualities. She is unattractive, a tipler, wholly bad.

In many ways *Juan José* is a remarkable contribution to the Spanish theater. A departure from the familiar middle class *mores* found in nearly all the plays of the nineteenth century —the "comedias de costumbres", especially— it represents a new trend, broadening the scope of Spanish drama to a greater extent than ever before.

Significant as social drama and also indicative of Dicenta's interest in the lowest economic groups in Spain is *El señor feudal*. This three-act drama in prose was first presented in the Teatro de la Comedia, December 2, 1896. The setting: just outside Roque's farm home one hour before sunset.

Roque has risen by hook and crook, and other devious means, to a position of wealth. He has gradually taken everything his former employer, a *marqués*, had except a castle and his niece, María. What is more, he holds a 10,000-duro mortgage on the former and hopes to marry his son Carlos to the latter. On a promise of marriage, Carlos has seduced Juana, the daughter of Juan, the old foreman on Roque's finca. Roque asks the *marqués* for María's hand in marriage to Carlos and the nobleman, refusing, laughs at his former stable boy. María, on the other hand, out of love for her guardian, convinces the *marqués* that she really loves Carlos (hating him all the while), planning to marry him and thus be able to support her uncle in his old age. Juana's brother Jaime returns from eight years study in Madrid, learns of the situation, and promises Juana that Carlos will marry her or no one. It is harvest time and the huge wine vat in Roque's cellar must be filled. But, ere this exhausting chore can be accomplished Jaime challenges Carlos either to marry Juana or die, and when Carlos refuses to marry her, Jaime throws him into the wine vat. He locks the door, and presents Roque the key. Roque feels exalted having achieved all he set out to do. Upon entering to supervise the filling of the vat, he arrives too late to save his son's life.

Stark melodrama from the interesting opening scene to the dramatic finale, *El señor feudal* is typically Dicenta. It deals with the lower classes of farming folk who eke out a bare existence working in all weather from fifteen to eighteen hours a day. All of the harsh conditions are graphically described by the consciously purposeful author, yet not so much in detail that interest in the plot lags. Here is a case in which a laborer through dishonest practices has attained to greater position than he deserves at the expense of all who work for him, and finally is given his "comeuppance" by the members of the same group whence he sprang, in the loss of his only son. The treatment is novel in that, whereas Dicenta in other plays, and other playwrights, too, preferred to take a stand against the established bourgeoisie who exploited the workers to maintain their *status quo,* Roque represents a new group who need to be reminded of their origin from time to time.

In this aspect of oppression and exploitation *El señor feudal* constitutes social drama. An ironic twist is Dicenta's choice of a *parvenu* to represent the *señor feudal* instead of the *marqués* who really is a dignified, kindly, ideal type of old nobleman in comparison with whom Roque and Carlos are scoundrels. Attesting to this is the sincere attitude of respect which the laborers feel for the *marqués* and María, whereas the newcomers are only feared for their brutishness.

The idea of melodrama is further extended in María's being forced to marry the son of Roque, the mortgage holder, to save her guardian's life. With few changes this play might pass for showboat drama in the United States of the same period.

Interesting, too, for its implications, is Jaime's return to the farm from the outside world of culture and opportunity in the big city. He has learned about life in his difficult study period away from home, and acting as *raisonneur,* he is able to achieve a bystander's viewpoint of the oppression of the peasant as typified by Roque's and Carlos's treatment of his family. In his conversations with Juana and his reactionary father, who fears to try to change the situation, preferring to cling to the traditional way, Jaime depicts the idea of progress, which can only be achieved, the author attempts to indicate symbolically with the vat scenes, through violent action. It would be stretching the point to declare categorically that the play is revolutionary, advocating overthrow of the existing government, but *El señor feudal* is not simply an evening's entertainment. It is more important than that. The least perspicacious of the audience must have recognized Dicenta's attack on oppression and exploitation of the peasant farmer.

As usual with Dicenta's works, the play is heavily weighted with symbolism. Jaime represents the idea of progress, while Juana and Juan are the downtrodden mistreated peasants having to endure and afraid to try to change matters, completely subject to the overlord. Together with the minor characters of the *finca* workers they constitute a bloc opposed, but not actively so, to the exploiters Roque (now *don Roque*) and Carlos. In connection with this is the very effective symbolism of the vat or *cuba*, which every harvest season must be filled with new wine for Roque's cellar. Highly symbolic is the scene in which the workers are shown again and again all day long bringing in the heavy barrels of wine and pouring it as if into a bottomless container that, it seems, will never be filled. All of the description of this scene becomes particularly effective in the next to the last and the last scenes where Carlos is murdered and Juana is avenged, and Jaime presents the key to the vat now filled, at last, to Roque. This is original and must be a sensational scene in presentation. It does recall Echegaray's technique in the long and steady build-up in preparation for the big scene in the last act. There is enough here to appeal to the sensation-seekers and pack them into the theater for nights to come.

In developing the vengeance motive Dicenta resorts to Golden Age technique and thus satisfies the traditional demand for terrible punishment of the seducer. This incident is not in keeping with the theme of progress which underlines the drama, but it is strikingly melodramatic and thus, in the eyes of the theater managers, is justified.

The characters are not as clearly delineated as they are in *Juan José*. There is not one great individual. Jaime is not enough in evidence to become the giant that Juan José is. Roque himself is not so described as to make the audience align itself wholeheartedly against him, while Carlos is simply a poor or faded copy of his father, wholly undistinguished. Indeed, there are so many minor characters that all are blurred and indistinct. None is overdrawn for emphasis or contrast. In summary the play would be effective particularly for its colorful and sensational scenes and scenery. It is not profound, but there is enough of the dramatic in the plot to make it interesting.

The play which reveals to the greatest extent Joaquín Dicenta's naturalistic tendencies and the Zola influence in Spanish drama is *Daniel*. This four-act prose drama was first presented in the Teatro Español, March 7, 1907. The scene: the *talleres* and *dependencias* of a mine.

The miners have a very hard lot, the owners and the army having quelled completely any uprisings and demonstrations designed to improve wages and conditions, and another act certain to provoke violence, a wage-cut, is in the offing. When it is announced, the miners, led by Cesárea, the "Apóstola" who had lost her husband in a battle with the troops called out to protect the mine, go out on strike. Daniel, a fifty-five-year old, who has spent his life working in the mines, has two sons. One of them works in the mine; the other is in the army. In a misguided attempt at retribution for their suffering the miners destroy much of the mining machinery and try to prevent the *esquirols* (workers brought in from other areas) from working the mine. Spurred on by the mineowners, the troops fire on the strikers, and in the fight both of Daniel's sons are killed. In Act IV Daniel, a cripple since their death, is guard at the mine elevator. The owners and several guests go down to one of the lower levels of the mine to have a picnic. As the owners are coming up in the elevator, Daniel releases the safety lever, and all the capitalists plunge to their death in the mineshaft.

In this violent, action-filled drama Dicenta's purpose seems really revolutionary. *Daniel* is perhaps one of the strongest attacks on capitalism ever to reach the Spanish stage. The entire play is heavily slanted in favor of the workers, frequent reference in great detail being made to their plight: thirteen-year-old boys working in the mines pushing heavy carts filled with molten lead; women working alongside the men, women grown old before their time because of the harsh conditions at the mine; the maiming and even murder of many of the miners due to inadequate safety practices; and slaughter perpetrated upon them whenever they make any efforts to better their situation.

Dicenta had so gone over to socialism by this time that the play has nothing good to say for the wealthy classes, and his case against them is emphatically one-sided. This argument is brought out in the author's portrayal of Daniel. The *obrero* is described throughout the play as long-suffering, clinging to established customs and practices, defending the mine owners and saying that life is like this: the rich become richer and the poor have to work. He even defends his smelting furnace when the strikers come into the plant to destroy the machinery. And when they wrest his tools from him, and lead him away, he weeps. Daniel recalls Juan in *El señor feudal*, who strove to maintain the *status quo*. Daniel's attitude does not seem to change in any way until the final scenes when he discloses his long-considered plan to wreak vengeance upon the mineowners, because they have been instrumental in destroying his family: his wife, who died of malnutrition, both sons killed in the fracas at the mine, and his only daughter become now the *querida* of Luis, the mine-owner's son. The audience is in for a severe shock on the nervous system —perhaps the incident which they looked forward to and which Echegaray-like had brought them to the theater in the first place. But the elevator-releasing event is so completely unprepared for that the astonishment is perhaps too great. It is sensational, spine-tingling, superficially emotional, but hardly the best example of dramatic technique. *Daniel* is symbolic. According to the philosophy of Dicenta the worker must resort to violence as his only recourse. As to the effectiveness of the play as a vehicle of social reform it is impossible to say. As a work of art it is not outstanding. What purports to be a capitalism vs. labor argument or a social reform movement advocating improvement of the workers ends as a shocking melodrama, the resolution too sudden for acceptance.

As has been suggested, the Echegaray influence is apparent in the plot, in the characters, and in the situations. Especially is this true in the tableau at the end of Act III showing Daniel standing helpless between the bodies of his two sons. The irony of brother against brother in the incident at the mine may have been inspired in *Germinal*, Zola's novel. Certainly the wealth of detail in description of the mine is naturalism in the extreme.

Though *Daniel* is interesting enough, as a dramatic piece, it is clear that Dicenta's chief purpose was social reform. And to intensify his aims, which are ever obvious, Cesárea, the *raisonneur*, at various times recounts incidents which are the basis for her determination to change existing conditions, declaring again and again that, though she loves one of the workers who loves and wants to marry her, she cannot give up her one purpose in life even for him. She won't jeopardize her chances for accomplishing her objective by dividing her attentions. Brave and forceful, Cesárea states the position of the worker, but indicates little hope for early success: "Es precisa la muerte no sólo nuestra, sino también las de miles y miles de hombres para el bien de los que nos sucedan."

In a way, actual details of plot and background are only of incidental importance in *Daniel* and in other Dicenta writings. The social doctrine whose vehicle they were is, for the author, at least, much more significant. Zola was a major influence in the spiritual formation that produced the social concepts voiced by Dicenta. The proof and symbol of this fact is Dicenta's editorship of the Madrid weekly *Germinal*.

This journal first appeared April 3, 1897, as an organ of Naturalism in literature and Socialism in politics. According to its program, "Germinal" would devote itself chiefly to economics and social problems, "cuyos pavorosos conflictos describe el gran poeta francés en su inmortal obra Germinal". Dicenta transferred his allegience not long afterward to *El País, Diario Republicano Social Revolucionario,* but only to address a wider audience in work of the same nature, written under the same spiritual auspices. Zola might well have disowned the violent partisanship displayed in *Daniel* and other plays of Dicenta, and seen Naturalism only in their documentation, but when the name "Germinal" became for Dicenta a symbol of his creed, the great naturalist's responsibility can scarcely be denied.

It is well known that Dicenta frequently borrowed from Dicenta. As to Dicenta's methods of recasting material, it is interesting to speculate upon the psychology of that method, the compulsion Dicenta seems so often to have been under to work fields already harvested rather than new ones. The most satisfying hypothesis is that Dicenta was and remained at bottom a journalist, in whatever form he expressed himself. His were certainly not the motives that led Galdós to repeat himself. Never in Dicenta's double treatment of a theme is one version a pendant of the other, as *Realidad* is of *La incógnita*. Never is it felt, as with Galdós's stage adaptations of dialogue novels, that the problem of medium concerned him. His was not even the rewriting in different form of a popular work, a *Doña Perfecta* or a *Gerona*. Dicenta merely seems to have found creation difficult without a sketch to work from. And the sketch, if one accepts the untypical first drafts of untypical *sainetes* and musical plays, is usually journalistic, and probably always written for publication, in a newspaper. Thus to the artist's having borrowed from journalism, to the editor's near incapacity to refrain from voicing his partisan views, is added the reporter's disinclination to depart from fact. And all support the hypothesis that whatever his relative merits and fame as dramatist, novelist and newspaperman, Dicenta and the latter rarely parted company.[2]

In conclusion, Joaquín Dicenta enlarged the scope of Spanish drama. He continued the Echegaray tradition while developing new fields. His dramatic works, the greatest of which have been studied here, are frequently intriguing, though not often profound. Sometimes very dramatic, his plays depend largely for their resolution on sudden shifts of plot and startling surprises. The social emphasis is the more important interest in Dicenta's playwriting.

The greatest novelist of the nineteenth century in Spain turned in later life to the drama. Benito Pérez Galdós (1843-1920), the author of many "Novelas contemporáneas" dealing with social problems, enjoyed perhaps greater success with "Episodios Nacionales", his panoramic history of Spain in the nineteenth century. The literary giant who averaged more than a novel a year for all of his long productive life found time to produce also

---

[2] EDWIN S. MORLEY: *Hispanic Review*, vol. IX, 1941, pages 383-393.

some twenty-one plays, several of which represent a worthy contribution to the field of social drama.

The earliest of these to appear was *Realidad*, "arreglo de la novela del mismo título", a drama in five acts, in prose, first presented in the Teatro de la Comedia, March 15, 1892. It had a rather exceptional run, being presented on twenty-two consecutive evenings.

Federico Viera is the lover of Augusta, the wife of Tomás Orozco. Federico's life has been one seduction after another, and his reputation is well known. Federico's aspirations are aristocratic, but he has no money, and of course cannot, must not, work. This would be beneath his dignity. He has a sister Clotilde, who loves a *tendero's* son, and class-conscious Federico makes their lives miserable trying to keep these two apart. Federico, in order to live, is reduced to borrowing from a former mistress Leonor, "La Peri", a demimondaine. This is a loan about which he wants nothing to become known, of course. Incidents are provided in abundance to show the opposite character of Orozco, kind, generous, and charitable, who cleverly and legally outwits Federico's negligent and unscrupulous father Joaquín in order to get money for Federico and Clotilde. Augusta loves Federico, and goes to see him, now reduced to poverty, to offer to help him.

But Federico is quite beside himself with worry and remorse, having betrayed his benefactor so often that this time he must refuse for the sake of "honor" the money Orozco offers him. And at the end of Act IV Federico steps offstage into his "bedroom" and shoots himself. In Act V much shorter than any of the others, something like an epilogue, Orozco comes to realize his wife's unfaithfulness, and in his own mind regards her as dead. And, indeed, it is evident that she has now lost everything. Ever-kind Orozco forgives Federico, who appears fleetingly as a ghost at the end of Act Five.

In this long drawn-out, extensively philosophical and psychological play, the brilliant novelist Pérez Galdós essayed for the first time the field of the drama. But the play was not an unqualified success. Criticism varied. His detractors strove valiantly to condemn the play. Nevertheless, a run of twenty-two nights would be significant of its effect, disregarding its authorship and what Galdós's admirers did to keep it on the boards. Though there was much adverse criticism, newspaper articles seemed to weigh the balance slightly in favor of the play. The acting was not as competent as Galdós and the audience might have hoped for, and the audience must have been exhausted when the curtain fell on the last act, because *Realidad* is extremely long.

Realidad is a synthesis of two novels *La incógnita* and *Realidad*, the latter already fairly popular as a dialogued novel. Unfamiliar with stagecraft, having been so absorbed in his novel-writing that he either had no time for the stage or until the nineties did not feel any inclination for it (for some twenty years he had not been in a theater, contemporary commentators declared) Galdós had to devote many afternoons to personal observation of theatrical performances, and while writing, or rewriting *Realidad*, spent a long time familiarizing himself with the details of the stage. Needless to say, it was with great fear and concern that he witnessed its first performance. He had much at stake. But his concern was unnecessary. Though the first act received only mild acclaim, the second little more, the success of the third was attested to with unrestrained applause. And when the play was over, Galdós was established as a new force on the Spanish stage.

Realidad is social drama on a new and philosophical plane. Not that the drama immediately preceding 1892 was not to some degree philosophical. But Galdós's treatment of the problem of adultery is more profound than that usually accorded this oft-used device on stage, different, and, with regard to his departure from the customary Echegaray technique of terrible vengeance exacted by the outraged husband, modern in the extreme. In this respect does Galdós differ most from his predecessors, indicating in addition to a desire to promulgate this new dramatic form, his sincere interest in progress and the betterment of Spain.

The plot is over complicated, making the play much too long. Certain columnists admitted that some articles of criticism written after the *estreno* were vague because they had to be written so late at night that the writers were unable to think clearly. This, of course, is not entirely true, but it is indicative of the attitude toward *Realidad* in certain quarters. Certain critics attacked its naturalistic tone, saying that some squeamish ladies in the audience could not stand the affront to Spanish *mores*, yet there is nothing in the play which could offend anyone in modern times. It was simply that some sectors of the audience resented this apparent intrusion of influence from the north—Zola, Ibsen, the Goncourts, et al. Galdós felt that realistic treatment was essential in drama of social implication.

The play by modern standards is not especially good drama. It is too heavy, too slow, and not characterized by much action. The dialogue is generally effective and real, but, if the audience got home by four a. m., much of the play had to be cut, and much of it could have been excised without loss. As to Galdós's dramatic technique, it is generally *llana*. In *Realidad* motivation seems obscure at times, as well as the interrelationship of certain characters.

Yet it is in characterization that Galdós attains his highest degree of success. The contrast between the two excellent characterizations of Tomás Orozco, Augusta's husband, and Federico Viera, her lover, is remarkable. Orozco, the philanthropist, an aristocrat, yet possessed of some democratic ideas as represented by his willingness to take Clotilde into his home as his ward, when her own brother, his aristocratic sensibilities outraged, had deserted her, unable to take care of himself or her, is diametrically opposed to Federico in characterization. Not only is Orozco philanthropical, but the exquisite irony of the play lies in Orozco's generosity being directed toward this Federico, the betrayer, the man who is living with his wife. This is the originality, the newness, the genius of Galdós. It is only in some of the details, which reflect his lack of experience, that Galdós errs.

In addition to its lengthy run in 1892 in Madrid, Barcelona, and on the road, *Realidad* was revived in February 1904. But time had apparently failed to increase the taste of the Spanish theater-goers for preponderantly philosophical and psychological drama. Orozco, the man of advanced ideas—the Spanish husband of tomorrow—was appreciated more than he had been in 1892, but he was by no means generally accepted. Reaction to him was in the nature of respect for an imported product; he was recognized by his resemblance to characters in the foreign dramas that occasionally came to the Spanish stage. Against the other innovations of the play the deep-rooted traditionalism and conventional taste of the public asserted themselves unmistakably. The audience, bourgeois for the most part, was as shocked as the spectators of 1892 by the few highly realistic scenes, and in general received the drama with dignified coolness. In only one respect had Spanish dramatic art progressed since the première—the reviewers seemed more intelligent. The critics ruefully bewailed the esthetic provincialism of Spanish spectators and no longer questioned the wisdom or soundness of Galdós's innovations.

Spanish audiences enthusiastically patronized the so-called "daring" plays by foreign authors—"daring" not in the philosophic or moral sense of the word, but in their defiance of priggishness. Why, then, the frowning attitude toward Galdós? To a few critics in 1892 and many more in 1904 it appeared that the author of *Realidad* was a leader whose stride was too long for the public taste; his concept of the drama was beyond the reach of the average intelligence. They could only hope that, for the good of progress in general and literature in particular, the Spanish public would some day soon catch up with Galdós.[3]

Though, as has been said, criticism varied, and there was a great deal of adverse criticism, including that of the Catholic Church and certain prominent laymen, favorable criticism always came from intellectual groups. For example, Leopoldo Alas ("Clarín") has this to say about Galdós's first dramatic effort: "*Realidad* presenta una saludable innovación, es una batalla ganada al convencionalismo y una puerta abierta a la realidad, a la idea profunda, a la psicología representable. El quinto acto de *Realidad*, donde sigue el drama que se había acabado (según receta antigua) en el acto cuarto, ese final es de un vigor, de una intensidad estética, de un patos realista y noble, que no tienen semejantes en la escena española."[4]

One of the best known of Galdós's dramatic works, also a dialogue novel, which had been published in October, 1892, is *La loca de la casa*. This *comedia* in four acts, in prose, was first presented in the Teatro de la Comedia, January 16, 1893.

---

[3] BERKOWITZ, H. C., *Pérez Galdós: Spanish Liberal Crusader*, The University of Wisconsin Press, 1948, pp. 260-261.

[4] GAMERO, E. G., *Galdós y su obra: Teatro*, vol. III, Madrid, 1935, page 19.

Jaime and Daniel, the two sons of the Marquesa de Malavella, are in love with Gabriela and Victoria, daughters of Don Juan de Moncada, a charitable civic-minded individual. José María Cruz, "Pepet", formerly a servant on Moncada's estate, returns wealthy from America, ambitiously hoping to marry Gabriela. But she flatly refuses. Cruz has acquired nothing but money, is completely lacking in social graces, and is vulgarly proud of his rise to fortune. Victoria, who is about to enter a convent, comes to spend her last two weeks, before her profession as a nun, with her family. Moncada is bankrupt, and Cruz will restore his business to its former success, if he can marry one of Moncada's daughters. Victoria is eager to accept the regimen of the order of nuns, is something of an ascetic, believes in mortification of the flesh, etc., but Moncada suggests he needs her with him now. Cruz, in his crude, tactless though honest manner tells Victoria he cannot understand how she could want to become a nun. But she is firm in her desire to sacrifice herself. Why not do so by marrying Cruz? What greater sacrifice could there be? In Act Three Cruz and Victoria have married. The Marquesa de Malavella seeks a loan from Moncada, who sends her to Cruz and Victoria. Victoria has a check given her by Cruz to pay a coal bill for the factory. She is the accountant. So she gives the money to the *marquesa*. Cruz is furious on learning what she has done, and he fears she still is interested in Daniel. (Jaime and Gabriela are married.) Victoria reminds Cruz of the conditions under which she married him, and since a serious misunderstanding has arisen between them, she says she is going to her family home. But she really loves him and when she tells Cruz that she is pregnant, she is able to drive a hard bargain with him and make him conform to her humanitarian ideas.

In *La loca de la casa* Galdós reveals his interest in the fusion of the social classes. José Cruz proposes this idea in his conversation with Victoria, when the conditions under which he will lend Moncada money, seem harsh. "Of what use is money if it does not afford him (Cruz) the pleasure, the luxury of being generous? What greater glory than to join the past with the present, for those who rose rapidly through their own efforts; to unite with those who yesterday were powerful when he was humble; to possess that which formerly was so far above him?"

This is the Spanish underdog who is speaking, the man who is entitled to some recognition for having scaled great heights in the world of finance. Through this person as *raisonneur*, Galdós points out the chief lesson to be derived from this social drama. Nevertheless, there are other occasions when the author indulges in open propaganda. Cruz recognizes many of the evils of society which are often supported in the name of charity. He does not give alms, which is the same, he says, as protecting the institution of begging and fomenting vagrancy and vices. It is not to be regarded as compassion. He knows that wherever that seed (of charity) is sown, ingratitude is born. Pity demoralizes men. From this come sentimentality, disrespect for the law, the unwarranted pardon of criminals, the rise of fools, the power of influence, and expecting too much from one's personal reputation. Of course, these things are true to a certain extent, but Galdós's thesis is too much overdrawn for the sake of emphasis. Cruz is a little too severe, as is religious, self-sacrificing Victoria almost too generous, the author's thought being to unite these two forces for good for the betterment of Spain.

It is no secret that Galdós was a reformer, and his desires for the improvement of social conditions are sincere. He wrote plays seeking glory, but his doctrine is genuine: his art is not prostituted for financial gain.

La loca de la casa is a better play than *Realidad,* and this in spite of the fact that the thesis or social lesson is always in evidence in the later play. And, though Galdós disclaimed intentional symbolism, in the two characters through whom he demonstrates this thesis—Cruz and Victoria, he epitomizes two powerful forces then present in Spain: the rough proletariat which through its own efforts and ability deserves a chance to rise in the world, and the traditional, religious, conservative, established nobility. He would have the more fortunate group ally itself with the lower elements in order to continue the good traits of the two classes in coming generations. Otherwise stated, Galdós strove to point out the necessity for the good of Spain to unite the forces of progress with the established defenders of conventionalism. Galdós was not a revolutionist. He did not advocate the overthrow of order and the *status quo,* but he did recognize the urgent necessity of amalgamation, a point of view which at the time would naturally be misunderstood, refused, and rejected by the arch-conservative elements in Spanish politics.

Galdós does not often feel called upon to resort to the *coup de théatre,* associated with Echegaray and which made the latter's plays popular with a large segment of the Spanish theater-going public; yet the influence of that leader in exciting dramaturgy is sometimes apparent in the works of Galdós. Cruz is a giant of a man, eccentric, uncouth, but few steps removed from the plow, as opposed to a large group of people representing established high society, "solid citizens" who resented his intrusion. In this respect the character is not unlike Lorenzo in *O locura o santidad,* though of course in conception they are worlds apart, and in no sense is it suggested that Cruz is mentally unbalanced.

As to the devices employed by his predecessors, duels, murders, adulteries, in *La loca de la casa* Galdós does not resort to these, though Daniel does challenge Cruz to a duel, which Cruz refuses. The realist Galdós showing his impatience with idlers, has Cruz declare that if Daniel sought suicide he would lend him a gun! This harsh tone softens later, however, when Cruz offers to help Daniel, rejected by Victoria, to start anew in South America.

As to criticism of the play at its *estreno, La loca de la casa* was pronounced a fair success by some and more or less a failure by others. Not even the author's minor concessions to conventional dramaturgy were sufficient to insure unqualified approval. The final stage version was substantially shorter than Galdós's original text. Often pruned during rehearsals, even with Echegaray present as consultant, the final result was of uneven merit.

Nevertheless, though the reactions of reviewers were widely divergent, jubilation was so great in Galdós's camp that it attracted new recruits. One critic, José Ortega y Munilla, formerly hostile, hailed Galdós as a courageous reformer and the new drama as a revolutionary milestone. At last, shouted the zealous convert, an intelligent public was born in Spain. [5]

---

[5] BERKOWITZ, H. C., *Galdós: Spanish Liberal Crusader,* University of Wisconsin Press, 1948, page 264.

An instant and sensational success was *La de San Quintín*, a three-act *comedia* in prose, presented in the Teatro de la Comedia, January 27, 1894.

Of humble origin, but now wealthy, eighty-eight-year-old Don Juan Manuel de Buendía, with his son César, lives in a fine home in Ficóbriga. The Marqués de Falfán de los Godos, in debt to César, comes to see them. Also present as a guest is Buendía's niece Rosario, the Duquesa de San Quintín, formerly well-to-do, now poor. Víctor, thought to be César's natural son, who has studied abroad and is something of a socialist, is an *obrero* in one of his father's factories, for César is trying to break his independent spirit before he legally recognizes him. Víctor recognizes in Rosario the woman he had once seen in Belgium, whom he has adored ever since. César repeatedly asks Rosario to marry him, but she repulses him. She tries to make herself useful and does so in helping with the care of the house. She is not too proud to do her part. Falfán and César do not get along, and when the former gets possession of some love letters belonging to César, he gives them to Rosario to pass on, as if by mistake, to César. Rosario's motives in agreeing to such a conspiracy are twofold. Having fallen in love with Víctor, she would like him to prove his independence of the Buendía family. She is also angry at César. The information contained in these letters is proof that Víctor is not César's son. In an effort to hurt César and get even, she presents the letters to him. César orders Víctor to leave, planning to send him to the United States. Rosario really loves Víctor, and when he tells her he wants to marry her, she gladly accepts.

This is another play in which Galdós pleads for a mixture of the good elements of the social classes in Spain, and *La de San Quintín* is an improvement over his earlier social dramas. Expressing Galdós's hopes for the amalgamation of the social classes, the strong, ambitious, honest, intellectual Víctor, something of a *raisonneur*, representing the author's ideas on truthfulness and honesty (these virtues to be practiced at all times in the face of any odds), is to combine forces with the proud aristocratic experience of the sound established nobility, and the two to work together for the good of Spain. This is Galdós's idea as exemplified in Rosario and Víctor, and, in spite of family opposition, they plan to marry. The fact that they intend to settle in the United States will not help Spain very much, however.

This play repeats the ideas of the previous one, in that it propounds a blending of the old and the new. In the former, however, it is philosophies which are involved, while here it is the mingling of the classes.

Galdós was now at the pinnacle of his success. Having attained unusual fame throughout the civilized world as a novelist, he had proved to the doubting Thomases among his harshest critics that he could also write good plays. Fifty consecutive performances of *La de San Quintín* in Madrid and a number of happy parodies constituted indeed an impregnable fortress of popularity.

His next play of note was *Voluntad,* a three-act *comedia* in prose, *estrenada* in the Teatro Español, December 20, 1895.

Don Isidro Bermejo is about to lose his store, through having guaranteed someone who failed in business. Foreclosure is imminent. He is suffering from *abulia.* Two of his children are useless in the crisis, engrossed in their own interests — Serafinito in sociology, Trinita in music. Doña Trinidad, the wife, is as useless as these two. They all wish that they had the other daughter, Isidora, back again. Isidora, however, had disgracefully left home to live with the rich Alejandro, who is not industrious. Nicomedes and Luengo pretend to be friends of Isidro, but actually they have an interest in getting possession of Isidro's store. About the time that things are becoming intolerable for Isidro, he learns that Isidora wants to come home. This news is brought by Isidora's brother Santos, who has just come to town. She comes back, is forgiven, and plunges into the work of rehabilitating the household, making everyone do his share of the work. Alejandro shows up and almost causes Isidora to spoil a business deal. She pulls herself together, however, and by a lucky coup, buys the *camisería* of Rodríguez, which Nicomedes had also wanted to buy. Alejandro meanwhile, has been ruined financially, and he is shattered by the news, delivered by Isidora. Her strong will prevents him from committing suicide, and the prospect of a happy life with Isidora revives him. He now even wants to marry her, a thing which he had previously objected to doing. The parents accept him on this basis, and all ends happily. In the last line of the play

Isidora says, "¡Oh! ¡Preciosa fuerza del alma! Aquí la tengo, aquí. Contigo he de hacer aún grandes cosas."

As is at once observed, Galdós here makes his first attack on that eternal failing of Spain throughout her history in modern times: *abulia*. This theme was to become popular among the Spanish *progresistas*. Notable in this regard was Angel Ganivet García (1865-1898), who perhaps was inspired through knowledge of Galdós's efforts to write his *Idearium español* (1896), well-known and much esteemed for its fine analysis of Spanish character. He concludes that Spain's chief fault is *abulia*, or weakness of will; hence the doctrine of *La voluntad*.

The *comedia*, not characterized by a great deal of action, might be reduced to this: an energetic young woman saves her family from financial ruin, and improves her own status from that of mistress to that of wife, rescuing at the same time her lover from complete lassitude of spirit. The plot interest is heightened by effective dramatic situations without the *coups de théatre* present in other plays by Galdós and even to a greater extent by members of the Echegaray school. Of course, the most obvious weakness of *Voluntad* is the implausibility of Isidora's financial genius in resurrecting her father's business without any previous experience. Overlooking this glaring failing, the plot is acceptable and usually interesting.

One of the most typical Galdosian devices is his advocacy of progress. Galdós was ever a partisan of action. It is necessary to act to get things done. In this play activity is seen to enter a place where there is inactivity, and the result is the more abundant life for all. This activity emanates from Isidora, and one might therefore expect her to be rewarded for bringing happiness to others. This is not the case to any degree, however, for certainly Alejandro does not appear to represent her whole happiness. He seems, rather, a liability. Isidora's happiness is achieved through winning it for others, and her activity brings its own reward in the satisfaction of doing good. Thus the play states the familiar principle that sloth and self-interest bring unhappiness.

Symbolism is evident in *Voluntad*, and it seems clear that the symbolism is intentional. Isidora stands for the effective and honorable exploitation of available resources, while Isidro represents the apathy of the past.

The lack of *vraisemblance* in the character of Isidora has been mentioned. Alejandro has something of the unreal about him also. It is true that both of them are unusual creations, but it seems that they are not wholly ethereal; it was for these characterizations that the critics ridiculed Galdós, but they deserve more praise than they received.

One may safely assume that in choosing to dramatize his popular novel *Doña Perfecta*, Galdós was moved chiefly by a desire to rehabilitate his waning dramatic fortune. The choice was a daring one. Aside from the potentially explosive theme, there was the uncertainty of the public's reaction to what it would be likely to regard as tampering with its property. For, whether accepted or rejected, this novel had succeeded in weaving itself into the spiritual texture of Spain. Moreover, by offering another dramatized novel, conceivably to reaffirm his doctrine of the fusion of the two techniques, Galdós once more defied the critics who insisted that it was this doctrine that was the root of his dramatic weakness. In any event *Doña Perfecta*, a four-act drama in prose, first presented in the Teatro de la Comedia, January 28, 1896, promised to be the outstanding theatrical event of the season.

Pepe Rey is an engineer on a mission in the region of Orbajosa, a town in the provinces. He is in love with his cousin Rosario. His aunt, Perfecta, is opposed to his interest in Rosario because she is convinced that as a scientist, he must necessarily be antireligious. She is aided and abetted in her animosity toward Pepe by the priest, Inocencio, great-uncle of Jacinto. María Remedios, mother of Jacinto, hopes to have her son marry Rosario. Pepe gets into disrepute in the town because of his supposedly irreverent behavior at mass, when he was admiring the artistic qualities of the church. To add to his "fame", Pepe and Tafetán, an older man-about-town, have been seen talking to some girls on the street. One of the girls is the sweetheart of Cristóbal, known as Caballuco, a local guerrilla chief. The country is torn by civil war, and in an effort to preserve the peace the governor has gained from Caballuco a promise not to take up hostilities. Pepe has a secret meeting with Rosario. It is interrupted by doña

Perfecta, who had locked Rosario in the house and would not let her see Pepe. He defies her. Their quarrel is ended by the noise of arriving troops. The army seems friendly to Pepe (among the troops he has found an old friend), and with his aid Pepe plans to run away with Rosario. Perfecta goads her local political friends into staging a revolt led by Caballuco. Pepe comes to Perfecta's house to see Rosario, and Caballuco is on the premises, on guard. When Pepe enters, María Remedios gives the alarm, calling out that someone is killing Perfecta. Then she cries, "¡Cristóbal, defiéndeme!". A shot is heard in the garden, presumably fired by Cristóbal. Someone falls. They pretend they do not know who it is, and his murder is left to appear accidental homicide. Doña Perfecta, her work done, says, "Misericordia, Señor, misericordia... para ellos... y para mí".

This play is perhaps the most involved one by Galdós yet examined. Yet it is much reduced in scope when compared with the novel. And in comparison with the novel, Galdós's real talent as a novelist becomes more evident. The novel far outshines the play in the matter of technique. It must have been a very difficult bit of work for Galdós to cut down one of his greatest novels, certainly one of his most controversial efforts —controversial enough to have been placed on the Index of books forbidden to Catholics— to a vehicle for presentation in less than three hours playing time.

Yet with all its weaknesses the play has several dramatic moments, and must have moved some members of the audience to recognize how terrifyingly deep-rooted the influence of the clergy had become in Spain at that time. And this influence, as Galdós has effectively pointed out, was not always for the good, or even intentionally good.

The symbolism of the characters seems greater in *Doña Perfecta* than in previous plays and the characters are even ironically named in the case of doña Perfecta and Inocencio, her spiritual adviser, that is, the church which was the real power behind Perfecta's vicious acts. Pepe Rey stands for progress, enlightenment, and the new order. Perfecta, on the other hand, dramatically opposed to him, represents obscurantism and tradition. The conflict is one between the old and the new. Had Perfecta not stooped to murder, she would have been a superior characterization, comparable even to some of the best of Shakespeare; and being identified with the ideals of the past, she might have reached heights of tragic grandeur. But by the action of the play we are forced to condemn Perfecta, and say that she stands for the wrong traditions, autocracy, and obscurantism, rather than for Christianity. She is an intriguing character. As is to be expected, the chief criticism of the play is that she is an exaggerated figure, but, done for emphasis this lends itself well to the effectiveness of the powerful drama. Poor Rosario, who is understood to be on the verge of insanity in the play and represents Spain in her inner conflict with her mother and her love for Pepe Rey, is caught in the middle, made to suffer because of the incompatibility of the two powerful forces.

Contemporary critics found the third and fourth acts something of a let-down after the *éxito sobresaliente* of the first two. The chief reason for this criticism is the removal of the important character, Inocencio, from the play. And it must be agreed that the author erred in this respect. Much time is taken in delineating the characters in the novel, making them unforgettable in the case of Perfecta and Inocencio. Perhaps, in the play Galdós toned down the development of the priest, the Penitenciario, lest it antagonize the church to a greater degree. But this does not seem likely, because there is still enough of what appears to be an attack on the church left in the play. Indeed this seems the essence of it. But it should be clearly understood that Galdós does not attack Christianity. The object of his literary shafts was obscurantism supported by members of the clergy, representatives of the church.

Doña Perfecta, as had been anticipated by the enthusiastic friends of the author, proved to be the outstanding theatrical event of the year. It was received less noisily than *La de San Quintín* had been, but the reaction of the audience was more intelligently critical. Attention was focused on the three main elements in the work: the fusion of the symbolism with the human interest of the love plot, the stature of Perfecta, and the role of the priest, Inocencio. For the first time in Galdós's dramatic career there was at least a semblance of harmony between public and critics. On the whole, Galdós had good reason to include *Doña Perfecta* among his noteworthy successes. It revived the general feeling that he was still a vital force in the reform of Spanish drama, and what was more important — it stimulated an intelligent reappraisal of the conflict between progress and conservatism in Spain on the eve of the twentieth century.

Curiously enough, old conservatives were at one with ultra-advanced youth in asserting that the theme of *Doña Perfecta* had lost its reality in modern Spain, except perhaps, in the backward provincial zones. The more reasonable opinion, however, was that the central national problem had remained unmodified, and that the only evidence of progress made in a score of years lay in the intelligence and objectivity with which the play was received. Most of the credit for this advance, it was alleged, belonged to the author.

It would seem that the revival of *Doña Perfecta* took Galdós back, artistically and philosophically, to the decade of the seventies, the days of his intense historical interest and symbolic realism. This required no effort on his part, since he had been gradually veering away from the realism of direct and minute observation toward the spiritual realities which were then the essence of continental thought. One could hardly say that any of his dramas thus far had dealt with ephemeral actualities. As a thinker he was slowly ascending the heights of idealistic contemplation and severe judgment. In 1876, when *Doña Perfecta* (the novel) was published, he had identified fanaticism with conservatism and reaction, and tolerance with liberalism and progress, and these he had in a sense interpreted as forces released by human institutions; now, in 1896, he was inclined to view fanaticism and intolerance as the result of one and the same spiritual pathology — tyranny. [6]

Doña Perfecta deals with a serious problem in Spain, though perhaps today it is not so much so as it had been. But at the time of the conception of the novel Galdós must have felt that the situation warranted attack, else he would not have attempted it. In the character of doña Perfecta we see encompassed all the terrible forces of reaction and the medieval directed against the

---

[6] BERKOWITZ, H. C., *Galdós: Spanish Liberal Crusader*, University of Wisconsin Press, 1948, pages 277-278.

idea of progress and improvement, and the force of this conflict is felt deeply and more and more frighteningly until the tragic climax is reached. The audience is made to feel the hopelessness of the situation to such a degree and so effectively that it cannot fail to identify itself with the character of Pepe Rey. The novel is more effective than the play, but with knowledge of the novel, one can better appreciate Galdós's dramatic effort and overlook the technical difficulties which lessen the author's success as a dramatist. *Doña Perfecta* remains a worthy contribution to the field of the drama.

As the nineteenth century gave way to the twentieth, Galdós once more became imbued with the missionary spirit. Something of this sort had in part motivated the resumption of the *Episodios Nacionales*, but he now felt that this was not an effective way of serving the cause. He was eager for more immediate contact with the people, and for this there was nothing better than the drama. And *Electra* was the drama that was to achieve the rebirth of Spain, Galdós hoped. This five-act prose drama was first presented in the Teatro Español, January 30, 1901. [7]

Máximo, nephew of don Urbano, is a successful scientist and a widower with two children. He lives next door to his uncle and aunt, Urbano and Evarista. Electra, daughter of a cousin of Evarista, lives with them. She is a madcap, but has a great capacity for seriousness and helpfulness when rightly governed. This, of course, is part of the symbolism of the play. Electra's mother, Eleuteria, was a wayward woman. There is a suggestion that Pantoja may be the father of Electra. He is an obscurantist and is the founder of San José de la Penitencia, a convent. He had been one of the loves of Eleuteria, who had repented of her past life and lived out her days at the convent Pantoja founded. Pantoja wants to expiate his past by getting Electra to enter the convent. At the same time, a family friend tells Electra that he is ill, and that he will see to it that she is taken care of. This is Cuesta, who suffers from a cardiac condition. Meanwhile, Electra and Máximo have fallen in love, starting by her befriend-

---

[7] BERKOWITZ, H. C., *Galdós: Spanish Liberal Crusader*, University of Wisconsin Press, 1948, pages 346-348.

ing his children and leading to her helping him in his laboratory. There is a great deal of elaborate symbolism here, dealing with the fusion of two metals in making an alloy. Pantoja is thus blocked in his efforts to get Electra into a convent. He tells Electra that Máximo is not the son of Lázaro Yuste and his wife Josefina Perret, but that Máximo's real mother was Electra's own, Eleuteria. This drives Electra mad. They take her away to La Penitencia. The *marqués*, a friend of Máximo who has helped their romance from the start, and Máximo himself, come to the convent to tell Electra that Cuesta has died and has left half his wealth to her if she will leave the convent. Pantoja, confident she will remain, says she is free to choose. The *marqués* and Máximo agree to take her away at once. They have keys to one of the gates, and one of the sisters will help them. This sister tells Electra that Máximo is on the way, and that her consanguinity with Máximo is deniable. Electra has a vision of her mother, of whom she has had other visions in the past. The vision tells her that her supposed relationship to Máximo is false, and that it is unnecessary for her to stay in the convent. The *marqués* and Máximo arrive and take her away, leaving Pantoja to his solitude.

There are three elements present—Máximo, representing material progress; Electra, representing the more imaginative side of this nature, and perhaps also the spirit of electricity if not of metallurgy, chemistry, and physics; and Pantoja, representing the forces of reaction. There is, of course, the suggestion that steady Máximo needs the help of the more volatile Electra at times. This recalls, of course, *La loca de la casa*. The central idea, however, judging from the action, is that obscurantism cannot retard progress.

The tumultuous reception of *Electra* was the Spanish version of the famous premiere of Victor Hugo's *Hernani*. The disillusioned Spanish realists of 1901 experienced something comparable to the frenzy of the French romanticists of 1830. Ramiro de Maeztu hurled the first thunderbolt with his outcry of "Down with the Jesuits!" During the third act the coldly intellectual and devastingly nihilistic Pío Baroja shouted: "The entire meaning of the earth has been revealed here!" Azorín was sufficiently unnerved to exclaim: "Enormously beautiful!" Luis Bello voiced the thoughts of his youthful *confrères* when he announced: "Now we have a man in whom I believe!" And Valle-Inclán, sworn enemy of emotion in art, was seen crying behind his shell-rimmed glasses. [8]

Electra was hardly as good literarily as all this enthusiasm would indicate. The sensational course of the play was obviously due less to its intrinsic merits than to the conditions that accompanied its presentation. Wittingly or innocently, Galdós had chosen the opportune moment. The immediate reaction to *Electra* was political rather than literary. The very night of the premiere politicians already saw in it evidence that the storm of opposition against reactionaries and clerics was gathering fast. And the storm increased in fury throughout its phenomenal run — in the capital alone it enjoyed eighty consecutive performances in the Teatro Español, followed by more than a score in Novedades.

According to Andrés Ovejero, *Electra* was one of the most universal dramas of all times. The heroine was of Shakespearean proportions —in the fourth act she reminded one of Ophelia— and Galdós equaled the stature of the English dramatist. Only ignorance or envy, or both, could henceforth prompt anyone to deny Galdós the title of dramatist and reformer of the Spanish stage. He may not always have been a master of the art, but in *Electra* he revealed himself as "a portentous example of wisdom" in theatrical architecture. The characters were an enduring contribution to his already crowded and marvelous gallery. As for the theme, Señor Ovejero, himself a young man, seemed to speak for the youth of Spain when he said: "*Electra* is not only a dramatic work of highly singular merit, but also a beautiful, brilliant, magnificent manifesto of the aspirations of the intellectual youth of Spain, which in its recent preparations for the battle against clericalism has discovered Pérez Galdós an indisputable leader." [9]

As has been noted, Galdós's proven admirers used extravagant language. José de Laserna argued, without supporting evidence, that *Electra* was Galdós's best drama and one of the very few supreme achievements of the contemporary theater anywhere. Its symbolism was commendably transparent, and even its two acts of

---

[8] *Ibid*, pages 350-351.
[9] OVEJERO, ANDRÉS, "Galdós en el teatro", in *El Globo*, January 31, 1901.

exposition deserved only praise: first, because their unwonted length was a technical innovation; second, because they were required by the magnitude of the theme. As for the famous fourth act, which sent the audience into an exhausting delirium, it was "grandiose, sublime, Shakespearean, exuberant with poetry and emotion, a perfect model of lofty thinking, deep feeling, and plain speaking." [10]

Azorín had this to say: "The real theme of *Electra* was something profound and human — the eternal quest for truth and the meaning of life. Máximo (science) and Pantoja (religion) think that they know the goal of life, but Electra herself is only perplexed and confused by these two contenders for her guidance. [11] Azorín saw *Electra* as the work of a great thinker, the plastic and picturesque expression of the conflict as he interpreted it.

Galdós's dream of a Spain redeemed through the sorrow and suffering of the protagonist of *Electra* failed to come true during his life-time, and it still awaits realization today. Thoughtful Spaniards like to regard this as evidence of the enduring reality of the conflict portrayed in this drama. In recent decades, whenever the challenge of political or spiritual reaction —the two are hopelessly intertwined in Spain— has been ominously loud, the forces of progress and enlightenment have frequently used *Electra* as their protective armor. Other Galdosian plays, particularly *La loca de la casa*, and *El abuelo* (to be examined later), have been revived more often, but none with so much faith in its imperishable spiritual significance as *Electra*.

One of the most popular novels (dialogued) that Galdós wrote was *El abuelo* (1897). A thesis novel, it would be suitable for the stage, thought the author. In five acts and in prose, *El abuelo* was first presented in the Teatro Español, February 14, 1904. It was so unqualified a success that it brought Galdós warm tributes from his colleagues, old and young. [12]

---

[10] DE LASERNA, JOSÉ, "Electra", in *El Imparcial*, January 31, 1901.
[11] MARTÍNEZ RUIS, JOSÉ, "Ciencia y fe", in *Madrid Cómico*, February 9, 1901.
[12] BERKOWITZ, H. C., *Galdós: Spanish Liberal Crusader*, University of Wisconsin Press, 1948, page 259.

The aged Conde de Albrit revisits his former estates, now under the domination of his daughter-in-law, Lucrecia, Condesa de Laín, and the management of former servants who have prospered. The count's son, Lucrecia's husband, has been dead for some time. The count suspects that Lucrecia was unfaithful to his son, and that one of the two granddaughters —Nell and Dolly— is really the daughter of an artist, Carlos Eraul. Albrit wants to know which is which, in order to make the right one heir at least to the name and traditions of the family, if not the heir to very much real property. He confronts Lucrecia with this question, but she defies him. He talks to the children, thinking first one, then the other, shows more indications of nobility. Dolly shows a talent for painting, which makes the count wonder if she has inherited it from her mother's lover. At the same time, it is Dolly who is kindest to him, and does helpful things for him. The *condesa*, the former servants, and townspeople, try to get the count to enter an asylum. It is Dolly who refuses to desert him in this dark hour. Senén, the insolent steward who has risen in the world, finally gives the count proof that Dolly is the one who is not his own granddaughter, and Lucrecia authorizes her confessor to tell the count the truth. The count then accepts the reality, saying that which endures is within, and that it is love which is eternal truth. The count's pride is humbled by the discovery, but he is compensated by the love of Dolly for him. He is therefore, as a proud man, taught a lesson in humility.

The count stands for the old régime. Dolly stands for unsuspected virtues among those who are not of noble blood, in other words, the new order. For the count, the old order is changing, just as his own position has changed. He finally has to accept the truth. On the one hand, then, is the count, standing for the best traditions of the past; he expects the ruling class to display virtues. On the other hand, the best promise of the future is that virtues will be recognized for their own sake. The best ideals of both sides, therefore, meet and conflict. In the count's acceptance of the inevitable there is an effect of nobility, a note of grandeur.

El abuelo enjoyed widespread fame. Everything in it related to Albrit and his love for his *nietas* is appealing. Their relationship —especially that of Albrit with Dolly, the illegitimate daughter— is described with feeling and understanding. It reveals the author's interest in the *desgraciado* element in the Spanish population. But of most importance —indeed, the very essence of the play, and in this lies his purpose— is the idea, so carefully developed, that good can come from people not of noble blood. The symbolism in Albrit's name, namely "Don Rodrigo de Arista-Potestad", reveals the personality of its possessor, a proud nobleman of ancient lineage, beset with the problem of choosing which of his two granddaughters deserves to inherit his name and traditions. As is frequently the case, Galdós has created in him an unforgettable character, one of his best characterizations in a long list of excellent ones. One feels that he really knows this scion of distinguished family as intimately as one of his own good friends. He is admirably concerned with his family fortunes, apparently so reduced in every respect. And on top of his financial ruin he is faced with the problem of illegitimacy, the bar sinister. His concern is real. There is no evidence of superficiality in his feelings. He must determine which is which. And when he does learn the truth, at first he is *vacilante, descompuesto, trastornado*. But he is assisted in his acceptance of reality by another quaint Galdosian creation, Pío Coronado, who is *cornudo y contento* —and that many times— who is the tutor of Nell and Dolly.

The moral lessons contained within the framework of *El abuelo* are abundant: forgiveness, gratitude, and patience among so many aptly illustrated. The whole play, while intellectually appealing, is at the same time a gentle homily guaranteed to please the audience.

The play is almost without defects. It is not over-long, and incidents described and set forth to show the various characters in their true light are effective, neither too numerous or too long, all contributing to produce a generally entertaining play, while expounding a moral lesson and an eternal truth.

A nice touch is Galdós's decision to depict Albrit as nearly blind. Besides making him more pathetic and deserving of compassion, this tragic fact effectively prevents him from being influenced in his decision by the external appearance of the two girls. He can identify them only by their voices and characteristic actions.

In summary, *El abuelo* seems a fitting conclusion to our study of Galdós, because it embodies all the best aspects of his especial ability, namely that of delineation and creation of characters. It is an improvement over some of his earlier works in dramatic interest because of the absence of *coups de théatre*. The solution of the play is always apparent, but the audience cannot fail to be interested in the manner of developing the action of the play toward its logical and expected conclusion.

As has been stated, Galdós, the great novelist, turned to the drama in the latter part of his career. He who had created and given such intense life to a whole world of characters, who had invented so many plots and played upon so many passions, how could he fail to essay the stage? His powerful mind, whose originality was never satisfied with the beaten path, attempted to break new ways in this field. In *Realidad, El abuelo*, and *Casandra* (1905), he initiated the dialogued novel, *novela dialogada*, or *novela en cinco jornadas*, and from this to acting drama was but a step. In fact, these three *novelas* were all revised and shortened for performance. The most notable of Galdós's plays of social interest are *Realidad; La loca de la casa; Electra*, the most notorious, but far from the best; *El abuelo*, in which a Spanish Lear rejects Spanish traditions of family honor; *Voluntad*, a bid for reaction against the national failing *abulia; La de San Quintín*, in which is recognized the value of work in restoring a family's fortunes; and *Doña Perfecta*, the author's most powerful attack against clericalism. In these dramas, as in the best of his novels, his far-ranging spirit explores the recesses of the human conscience with stimulating liberty of judgment. Only his technical weaknesses prevent him from ranking among the greatest dramatists; from lack of early training he never mastered dialogue and stagecraft.[13] For this reason his plays were never truly popular, and never founded a school, but the better portion of his plays opens vistas of suggestive thought beyond the range of almost any other Spanish drama.

---

[13] MÉRIMÉE, E. AND MORLEY, S. G., *A History of Spanish Literature*, New York, 1930, pages 532-533.

CHAPTER VII

CONCLUSIONS

Though this book treats a few plays of the last years of the eighteenth century and the first decade of the twentieth, only important plays of social implication and representative thesis plays written by playwrights of the nineteenth century have been seriously considered. Reviewed historically, the first notable example of ethical drama is that of Ruiz de Alarcón (1581?-1639). In several delightful comedies, his purpose is ethical, definitely didactic, and subordinate to the plot. Generally considered to be his greatest comedy is *La verdad sospechosa*, one of the best plays of the Golden Age, in which play the author cleverly and amusingly teaches a not-too-trustworthy young man a needed lesson in honesty. The lesson is given only slight emphasis in the play, the interest lying in the action and in the originality of the author in creating novel situations. Alarcón wrote chiefly to entertain, but in his plays he recommends good manners and ethical conduct.

The same theme is further explored and expressed in *Las paredes oyen*, a critical study of slander and a eulogy of honesty, where the honest suitor wins the girl, and the slanderer is given the *calabazas*. Of course, Alarcón's main interest was action, his plays intended to entertain, and in this purpose he was as typically Golden Age as Lope de Vega, Rojas Zorrilla, Tirso de Molina, Calderón, and the rest. But he differs from these other dramatic leaders in his preoccupation with ethics. Because this aspect is not typical of the seventeenth-century *comedia*, and thus seems a prediction of things to come, indeed is of the essence of the drama to be studied, Alarcón is mentioned here.

The seed of social drama did not find fertile ground in the eighteenth century. In fact, drama suffered serious decline in this period, and social drama, as was the case in the seventeenth century, was almost non-existent. In Spain two men, Gaspar Melchor de Jovellanos (1744-1811) and Tomás de Iriarte (1750-1791), contributed to this genre, yet in the embryonic stage. In 1774, Jovellanos presented *El delincuente honrado*, a mild complaint directed at Charles III's edict against duelling, in which the author describes the suffering of a fugitive from that law, a fugitive who was justified, according to the code of a gentleman of that day, in fighting the duel. In this play can be discerned the influence of the French *comedie larmoyante* and the *drame bourgeois*, the former a sentimental, tearful melodrama in verse, and the latter, in prose, noted chiefly for the moral lessons contained therein.

Contributing in a small way to the classical comedy of the eighteenth century, Tomás de Iriarte wrote two plays, similar to, and each the counterpart of the other: *El señorito mimado* (1788) and *La señorita mal-criada* (1788-1791). The titles clearly indicate the themes—that through his mother's over-indulgence of a young man's caprices he becomes unsuitable, or at least a poor risk, for marriage, losing out to a better-disciplined suitor; and, in the second play a young girl encouraged by her too complaisant father to be wilfully contrary misses her best chance for a happy marriage. These plays call attention to the need for the careful rearing of children, but the author supplies so many comic situations that the emphasis falls on entertainment.

In the nineteenth century, though actually belonging to the eighteenth in his cultivation of and adherence to the tenets of neo-classicism, the Spaniard who qualifies as the first to write good comedies in order to present a moral lesson was Leandro Fernández de Moratín (1760-1828). As one will notice, almost two-thirds of his life was a part of the eighteenth century. In Spain, owing to the despotism of Fernando VII, the nineteenth century as a division or segment of a literary movement really did not begin until his death in 1833, when involuntary exiles and emigrés returned to Spain, bringing the new ideas of Romanticism from the rest of Europe, but especially from France and England. Therefore, Moratín is representative of the eighteenth century.

In this respect, Moratín may be said to bridge the gap of the eighteenth century, from the ethical works of Alarcón to the nineteenth-century comedy of manners, which Moratín's later works seem to introduce. Moratín, though a classicist in his use of verse in his early plays, in his greatest *comedia*, *El sí de las niñas*, employed a very lively and expressive prose style, perhaps deeming prose more effective in the presentation of a moral lesson. In fact, this author is really a composite figure in the drama, because his works reflect the best traditions of the Golden Age, and definitely indicate a strong Molière influence, as well as foretell certain elements which were to occupy a place of importance in the nineteenth century.

Moratín's first play with a moral lesson was a tragedy *El viejo y la niña*, the title of which indicates the theme. The tragic aspect lies in the marriage of a *setentón* and a young girl having already taken place and thus it is an irrevocable act, an unpardonable crime perpetrated on an innocent child. In this play Moratín calls attention to the lamentable laws or customs which could produce this situation, and the play becomes a social document.

Believing undoubtedly that his talents lay rather toward the comedy, his next play was a *comedia*, *El barón*, taken from an original *zarzuela*, or musical comedy. From one extreme, the tragedy, the author leaps to the farce with probably the same degree of success. In this slight dramatic effort, his comic abilities become more evident, and some highly amusing scenes of rather low comedy, slapstick even, serve to give an imposter his "come-uppance". Also in the *Barón* Moratín introduces his most prominent theme of education for young girls. Judging from the lines in his plays, marriages between people of extremely different ages were not uncommon, and these marriages were usually effected through devious means and selfish designing on the part of an over-ambitious tutor or mother. Moratín challenges the morality of keeping adolescent girls in the dark about vital matters. Their parents seem to expect them to be completely subservient to their wills, the daughters to be granted no voice whatsoever in the most important event in their lives. The farsical tone of *El barón* keeps it from ever assuming any aspect of serious connotation, but the underlying theme is education.

This same theme appears in *La mojigata*, Moratín's "hypocrite" play, revealing again the Molière influence in its similarity to *Tartuffe*. Here a father has so influenced his daughter's way of thinking that she has learned to "think" as he expects her to do, but her real ideas, ideals, thoughts, and actions belie the lessons he has taught her. This play, too, has many of the elements of the farce about it: eccentric characters and gayly amusing incidents, not yet expressing the author's ideas on education in a serious manner. But they indicate a desire on Moratín's part for better education for a realistic life.

The best play that Moratín contributed to Spanish theater was *El sí de las niñas*. In this *Comedia*, his ideas on education attained fullest development. Here he presents a cogent argument for a better system of education when a fifty-nine-year-old man decides he should not marry a sixteen-year-old girl, whose mother was forcing her into the marriage for personal, selfish reasons. The man (Diego), so keenly must the author have felt on this subject, stops the play at several points, and at one time for many minutes, to present his (the author's) observations on such an unfair, immoral practice. The *raisonneur* assumes an importance here which was to continue throughout the century in the dramatic works of many of the later playwrights.

El sí de las niñas is the culmination of Moratín's abilities as evinced in his earlier plays. The happy combination of an interesting plot, the creation of at least two striking characters and a serious moral lesson is a rare and not-to-be-ignored event. As Larra said, his depiction of local customs and delicious satire combine to make Moratín's last play especially interesting. Of course, his concern with the local, the actual, and the need of a particular locale differentiates the works of Moratín from the universal art of Molière.

Typical of the neo-classical school, whose tragedy attained certain fame, but whose comedy really never existed in spite of Moratín's efforts, was Moratín's careful observance of the unities in all four of the plays studied. His most notable break with the custom of this school was his use of prose in *El sí de las niñas*. His social *milieu* was always the bourgeoisie, the class which made up the greater part of his audiences, we must presume.

That the play was worthy of presentation and perhaps exerted an influence on morality of the times is attested to by several contemporary and later references. Larra, deploring "locas bodas y desatinados enlaces", praised it highly in an 1834 presentation, calling for another Moratín to come forth and write another play to try to correct the sad state of moral life in Madrid in his day. Again in 1848, twenty years after Moratín's death, Ventura de la Vega wrote "La crítica de *El sí de las niñas*", a clever bit of dramatic criticism, a play within a play. And he, too, sings its praises, calling it "la joya del teatro moderno".

In Moratín can be seen, in his concern for morality and ethical conduct, the tradition of Molière and Alarcón as well as a suggestion of things to come, the *comedias de costumbres*, which were to fill the Spanish stage henceforth. His influence is apparent in the works of several playwrights of the first half of the nineteenth century. "Continuators of the Moratín tradition" we have chosen to call them.

The earliest of the playwrights of the "escuela de Moratín" was Francisco de Paula Martínez de la Rosa (1787-1862). Admittedly imitative of Moratín, this poet-statesman-playwright wrote three generally amusing *comedias* on various social failings. In *Lo que puede un empleo* (1812), Martínez de la Rosa presents social satire in a pointed and purposeful manner. This prose play attacks the hypocrisy and worldly ambitions of certain members of the clergy. The essence of the plot, extremely simple even for a two-act play, is a sermon on what lengths a man will go to to obtain a sinecure. In this play, a worldly priest who almost succeeds in breaking up a love match (because the young man is a "liberal"), with which the priest had no reason to concern himself. Martínez de la Rosa wrote this *comedia* while taking advantage of that period of unrest in the reign of Fernando VII, familiar to the student of Spanish history. One might say he used the times as a backdrop for his político-moral recommendations. He was, then, an opportunist. His purpose is commendable, advocating, in the course of his verbal attack on irresponsible clergymen, among other desirable privileges, freedom of the press. As Moratín had done, Martínez de la Rosa teaches his lesson through ridicule. The priest is taught a well-deserved lesson.

Reminiscent in great detail of the plot of *El sí de las niñas* is *La boda y el duelo* (1820). In plot, characters, and situations, Martínez de la Rosa's play seems an echo of Moratín's masterpiece. Of course, the copy is rarely as good as the original, and this adage applies in this case. Only one good point can be made in comparison in defense of the Martínez de la Rosa play, and that is that Carlos, the young lover, acts as a hot-blooded youth in love is expected to do. In this characterization, Martínez de la Rosa outshines his model. Otherwise, the play is a shadowy, pale imitation, without the grave feeling of the serious scenes and the natural humor of the minor characters so delightful in *El sí de las niñas*.

His best *comedia*—like the second, in verse—is *La niña en casa y la madre en máscara* (1821). The title indicates the substance of the play—negligence in the care and education of a daughter. The play thus continues the tradition of campaigning for a change in education practices as seen in the plays of Martínez de la Rosa's mentor, Moratín. The mother Leoncia, because of her lack of attention to the education of her daughter, is responsible for a situation which almost provokes tragedy. Reminding one of the character of the title role of Moratín's *El barón* is Teodoro, who almost abducts Leoncia's daughter while her gadabout mother is *en máscara*. As in his other *comedias*, which never attained the literary success of his moving and beautiful tragedies, Martínez satirizes various social failings, stopping the play on occasion, as Moratín had done, to pronounce his little homilies, notably on the inadequate, and in some cases, false education practices of the times. The play suffers from this excessive preaching and moralizing.

In the first and second plays Martínez saw fit to include the services of a *raisonneur*. In this respect, as well as in his observance of the unities, in the bourgeois atmosphere, and in his serious purpose, in the dramatic efforts of Martínez de la Rosa, the "comedia castigabat mores". The chief defect in the works of Martínez is the obvious imitation of Moratín, revealing his lack of originality.

One of Martínez de la Rosa's contemporaries, Manuel Gorostiza, was also writing comedies during this period. Not so seriously concerned with a lesson as Martínez de la Rosa was, Gorostiza, nevertheless, wrote several more amusing comedies designed chiefly to entertain, yet enclosing within the sometimes complex structure of their plots something which can be called a "thesis element". It should be understood, however, that Gorostiza can never be labeled as a "thesis dramatist". His purpose never was so pointed. It was with a spirit of fun and gay delight that he wrote such plays as *Indulgencia para todos, Las costumbres de antaño o la pesadilla,* and *Don Dieguito.* Each of these plays was written to provide a not too discriminating audience a couple of hours of entertainment, and that is the end of them all. But a slight moral lesson is present in each, though never in the least obtrusive. A discussion of these plays is included here, because Gorostiza may have had a secondary purpose in writing these comedies, perhaps prompted by a desire to use his talents to remedy the evils of society. The influence of neo-classicism (observance of the unities and the use of verse) and the tradition of Moratín are evident. And Gorostiza's plays are included here because they indicate the trend during the Romantic period toward the comedy of manners.

But comedy did not experience a real rebirth until the Romantic movement began. All the dramatists of the period wrote comedies, but all of them were eclipsed by Bretón de los Herreros (1796-1873).

Although Bretón was extremely prolific in his playwriting, his prime characteristics being fertility and variety, all his plays are very much alike. He wrote a long series of comedies with almost the same plot; *A la vejez viruelas, A Madrid me vuelvo, Un novio para la niña o la casa de huéspedes,* and *Todo es farsa en este mundo* for example. Bretón cleverly combines an unusual assortment of odd characters with a moral lesson to provide an entertaining though rarely moving—and never profoundly interesting—evening in the theater. All of these plays show the author's interest in society. Each of them purports to advise parents to give their daughters a chance to choose their husbands. But there is enough variety in the details to keep the usual audience entertained and frequently greatly amused, so much comedy is there in his plays.

The tone in each of Bretón's plays is ever optimistic. Bretón was not obsessed with a moral purpose in his plays. He usually exposes an eccentric suitor to embarrassing and often hilarious ridicule, and thereby teaches the girl's parents a lesson. Like Moratín and Scribe, Bretón depicts the bourgeoisie almost exclusively. His characterizations are slight. There is little time for excellent characterization in the Bretonesque comedy. His thesis comedy heroines are usually colorless. Sometimes a *raisonneur* is called into play, but his services are not usually required. Chance is also important. Like Gorostiza, Bretón serves as a bridge between the Moratinian comedy and the comedy of manners which was gradually developing into purposefully social drama.

Appearing soon after Bretón was Ventura de la Vega (1807-1865). Some elegant and clever verse, a few critical articles, and a certain number of plays assured his reputation. *El hombre de mundo* (1845), is the author's masterpiece. In it Vega attempts to show how a man's pre-marital escapades might possibly influence the success of his marriage. *The Man of the World* is based upon a popular proverb (Quien tal hace, tal lo paga), skillfully worked out in a plot that flows smoothly, naturally, and clearly; the dialogue is brisk and lively, and the rapid action quite properly veils the private opinion of the author, who lets the characters speak for themselves.

This "high comedy", that is, rather serious *comedia*, is a thesis comedy as well, a warning to roués and rakes to mend their ways, "donde un calavera que se ha casado siente la espina de los celos".[1] Vega continues the Moratín tradition in neo-classic observance of the unities and in his portrayal of the middle class. The subsequent thesis plays of Tamayo y Baus and López de Ayala were continuations of the high comedy of Ventura de la Vega.

By 1845, Romantic drama was all but dead; the clumsy imitators of that time possessed no fine qualities with which to compensate for the exaggerations of the school. The satiated public was quite ready to listen to jests at their expense, and the witty comedies of Gorostiza and Bretón de los Herreros did not miss their mark. There ensued a transition period of some ten years.

---

[1] HURTADO Y GONZÁLEZ PALENCIA, *Historia de la Literatura Española*, Madrid, 1943, page 886.

In this period, besides Bretón, stand Eguílaz and Ayala, who were destined to give a definitive form to modern Spanish drama. [2]

Tamayo is the author of several plays that were the delight of the Spanish public after Romanticism had lost favor. His works form a part of the European repertoire of the past century, being translated into nearly all the languages of the civilized world, and represented in the principal theaters of Europe and America. Tamayo occupies in Spanish literature a position equal to any attributed to his contemporaries.

He is the author of such plays as *Locura de amor* and *Un drama nuevo* which have caused his name to be praised beyond the boundaries of his own country.

The literary period of Tamayo extends from 1850-1870. Besides being a dramatist, he was also a moralist. He was constantly occupied with the study of social evils. Like Dumas *fils* he chose the theater as the most powerful literary means of direct action on public opinion. He claimed that literature should be a means to an end, that it should have in view the useful and the ideal. In his later plays he became an eloquent and bold moralist, who considered the theater the proper place from which to hurl polemics against impiety and vice.

Tamayo, with his moralizing temperament, had the dramatic instinct. He knew the resources of the theater, all the secret springs of the scenic art. He had a wonderful knowledge of the human heart and its passions. He understood the rules of composition, the wants and desires of the public. As he became more mature, his plays, though simple in form, showed more vigor. The plot is more concise, the number of personages in the play are reduced. His plays, in short approach more and more the classic type.

La bola de nieve (1856) is the first of Tamayo's thesis plays taken under consideration here. It is a study of the unhappy consequences of unreasonable jealousy, in which the author punishes the two individuals who err in their "celos infundados". This is the earliest of his real thesis plays, and it reveals the

---

[2] Mérimée and Morley, *History of Spanish Literature*, New York, 1930, page 526.

author's difficulty in establishing his form. The thesis is rather weak, and Tamayo has to force the plot and definitely caricature the opposing couples of good and evil to win his point. His chief weakness here is in character-delineation and development. The thesis is not of the same high social interest which his later plays revealed. The play is not to be completely condemned, because there are some realistic and dramatic scenes to recommend it, but his next drama is generally believed a greater achievement in dramatic technique.

In Spain, as elsewhere, the progress of democracy and science, and the increase of material resources in the nineteenth century, gave rise to a mad race for wealth. It was against this spirit, the greed for wealth which is demoralizing, that Tamayo protested in *Lo positivo*. The play has but little plot. The interest lies in the exposition of character and in the animated dialogue.

The Spaniards themselves consider *Lo positivo* ("cash") as one of their best comedies of manners. Though Tamayo got the idea from a French play, beyond this the play is original. The characters, customs, and the plot belong to the Spanish author.

Eminent Spanish critics give Tamayo high rank among Spanish dramatists of the nineteenth century. He tried to renovate the theater by introducing upon the stage plays with a decided moral element, and by giving to his serious dramas the didactic stamp which by degrees began to take root. We find there a spirit of observation and analysis, a scrutinizing study of the customs and manners of the time, as exemplified in *Lo positivo* and in *Lances de honor* (1863).

In *Lances de honor* the author makes a direct attack on the mistaken custom of duelling, of settling the most trifling matters on the field of "honor". And with the unprovoked murder of a young man in a "lance de honor", Tamayo shows clearly the terrible character of this custom so prevalent in Spain at the time the play was written. Unfortunately, in this play and in his money play, Tamayo weakens the dramatic continuity by including a *raisonneur* to expound his social ideas. Yet the inexorable force of this un-Christian custom of duelling remains an important factor in bringing about the ultimate dramatic and tragic conclusion. *Lances de honor* is a striking piece of dramatic literature, a worthy contribution to the field of social drama.

Los hombres de bien (1870) is another play in which a perceptive Spanish thesis dramatist sounded off against that saddest of Spanish failings: *abulia*. In this drama it assumes the form of excessive tolerance of vice, to an unreal and abnormal degree. So overdrawn (for emphasis) and so queerly delineated are the chief characters, that the play was a miserable failure. It was such a grievous shock to Tamayo that he withdrew the play after one night and wrote no more for the stage. Even a *raisonneur* in the person of an extremely noble character in opposition to the "honorable men" (a phrase used ironically), was not sufficient to rescue its social import from oblivion.

It will be observed that the character of the social drama is changing. Whereas, the early nineteenth-century playwrights seemed to want to return to a better period, recalling the "good old days", with Tamayo it appears that there is a different orientation, a forward look, anticipating a brighter future. The idea of the thesis play was growing.

Adelardo López de Ayala (1828-1879) was perhaps the greatest playwright still writing in Spanish at the date of his untimely death. Though his literary production is not large, his social dramas are of the most exquisitely polished compositions to appear on the Spanish stage from 1850-1880. It must be stated that his fame does not rest entirely on his dramatic or literary ability. He was a renowned statesman as well.

Throughout his collegiate career (1840's), Ayala was associated with Alberto Lista y Aragón, professor in the University of Sevilla, and this excellent teacher's conception of literature as a moral force wrought its influence upon him. His training here was probably influential in his persistent use of verse in his social drama, though by the 1860's this practice was regarded generally as outmoded. Ayala, like Tamayo, first wrote several successful historical dramas, but his greatest success lay in the four social dramas presented from 1856-1878.

The first of these was *El tejado de vidrio*, one of two Don Juan plays he wrote for the Madrid stage. In this one, the idea suggested in the title constitutes the admonition of the play, "That people who live in glass houses (and we all do) should not throw stones". Generally clever, the play is much lighter in tone than later thesis plays, because the Don Juan is not successful, he is taught a good lesson, and no one is hurt. The theme of the work is avowedly moral, for the author points out the danger to which the thief of another's property exposes himself, not considering that "todos los hombres tienen tejado de vidrio". It is the weakest of his thesis plays technically, and there are no distinguished characterizations. It continues generally the tradition of the bourgeois milieu, perhaps of a slightly higher social group of people from this same class. The author included no *raisonneur* here.

Like its predecessor, Ayala's second thesis play, *El tanto por ciento* (1861) is more concerned with action than characterization. One of two money plays, it is generally considered a worthy rival of Tamayo's *Lo positivo*, which was to appear soon afterward. *El tanto por ciento* is a satirical picture of society in Spain at that period. The mad money craze had been described in several plays by Scribe and Augier in France, and Ayala undoubtedly was greatly influenced by these two popular dramatists, whose works appeared often in Spain in translation. Ventura de la Vega and García Gutiérrez had done much of this kind of hack work.

The characters in *El tanto por ciento* are divided sharply into the two usual groups, strongly limned, and for emphasis either too good or too greedy. Curiously enough, Ayala's only *raisonneur* is the leader of the crooked money-grabbers, who, one is led to believe, by his moralizing speeches in the final scenes, seems called upon to expound the author's observations on society. This money play did not achieve the success enjoyed by Ayala's last and greatest social drama on a similar theme, *Consuelo*.

Ayala continued his study of the theme of the seducer in his next play *El nuevo don Juan* (1863), a comedy, yet, nevertheless, an attack on the Don Juan type. The environment of the characters of this play is that of the middle class. Just as was noted in the preceding drama, there is little character development. Actually, the main theme of the play is not the undoing of a don Juan, but the troubles and evils of jealousy. In many respects, this play is easily recognized as a *refundición* of a *zarzuela*, or musical comedy, by the author. Though Ayala thought the play "al nivel de las mejores mías", neither the contemporary public nor the critics agreed, and the play was a complete failure, because of the weakness in characterization and plot structure. The moral lesson is obscured by the comic elements in the play.

Ayala's last play was the one for which he is most famous both in Spain and abroad. *Consuelo* (1878) is primarily a character play. The personages are both interesting and poetic. All the important characters are of the middle class, and most of them are skillfully delineated and developed from the beginning to the end of the play. Consuelo, the protagonist, is one of those rare and unique character creations. The tragedy of her moral blindness is magnificently conceived and executed in this play. Because of her determination to marry for money and security, she loses the man who really loved her; and her husband is revealed as maintaining a mistress, for whom he deserts Consuelo. She wins her financial security and loses all else.

On analysis, the four social dramas are seen to be concerned with two themes, first that of the evil of the Don Juan, the seducer, and second the evil of speculation or devotion to money. The plays dealing with the first theme, *El tejado de vidrio* and *El nuevo don Juan,* are clearly not of so general a theme as the plays of the second group, *El tanto por ciento* and *Consuelo.* In his treatment of both themes, Ayala shows a similar tendency in the evolution of the development from the comic to the tragic. In *El tejado de vidrio* the Count is depicted as the vile seducer, though he comes to recognize his own weakness and repents. On the other hand, in *El nuevo don Juan* the author develops the character of the seducer after a more realistic fashion, for the play ends with the abasement of Don Juan and his proper ruin. In *El tanto por ciento* the protagonists are the victims of the money illness, and the play ends with their own happiness and triumph. In *Consuelo,* the protagonist herself is the victim of the malady and suffers because of it a tragic end.

The condemnation of the seducer developed in *El tejado de vidrio* and at greater length in *El nuevo don Juan* is clearly a reaction against the figure so favored by the romanticists, and so obnoxious in real life.

It seems certain that the questions which Ayala treated in *El tanto por ciento* and *Consuelo* were those of vital economic and social importance at the time of their appearance. The themes of the social dramas, which are certainly the best of the author's productions, could only apply to contemporary society, however, and with the passage of a few years lost much of their significance. But his concern with making the theater a powerful moral force plus his native and acquired dramatic skill, and his feel for the stage, combine to identify Ayala as one of the most outstanding nineteenth-century playwrights, not only of Spain, but of Europe as well.

While Tamayo and Ayala were contributing plays of social implications to the Spanish theater, Luis de Eguílaz (1830-1874), of the same school of moral dramatists, was writing thesis dramas. Unfortunately, the quality of his works does not measure up to the frequently lofty concepts which are to be found in the best plays of Tamayo and Ayala. Like them, Eguílaz strove to present a serious admonition to the Madrid audience in the plays he wrote. Most of his later works were little homilies in verse, while his earlier plays were edifying historical dramas, thus again paralleling the course of Tamayo and Ayala.

The three plays discussed in this book were chosen as exemplary of his social dramas. All are in verse, reflect a bourgeois atmosphere, are in a sense dramatic, and contain a moral lesson, frequently aided in its presentation by a *raisonneur*. The first, *Verdades amargas* (1853), is a slightly moving piece deploring ingratitude, though the oft-recurring phrase, "verdad amarga", like the preacher pounding the pulpit for emphasis, grows wearisome. The second, *Prohibiciones* (1853), of no greater dramatic appeal, advocates freedom of expression in one's choice of vocation as well as freedom of the press. And in these two there is little dramatic conflict to be discerned. Each play is a vehicle for Eguílaz's commentaries on society. Not entirely lacking in sentiment, each melodrama ends happily.

La cruz de matrimonio (1861) is a sentimental plea for the sanctity of the home, in which play the author also suggests that a woman's place is in the home. Though in part tragic, the repentance of a rake is brought about by his adoring and long-suffering wife in time to save their home. This play is very emotional, guaranteed to please the women who came to the theater for a good cry. Eguílaz's thesis, never profound, is propounded somewhat strongly, yet not always realistically.

In the same year that Eguílaz died another playwright, destined to enjoy greater success than that of Eguílaz, made his dramatic debut on the Madrid stage. This was José Echegaray (1832-1916).

The life of Echegaray, like every good Spanish play, is divided into three acts. The first shows us an engineer and mathematician, a professor and member of the Academy of Sciences; the second, a politician, free-trade economist and Finance Minister; the third, a dramatist, and this last capacity is the only one which gave him undying fame. Not until 1874 did his first play appear, *El libro talonario*. From that day on, one play followed another, and each opening night was a literary event. Among his sixty-three pieces of different types, one can separate those backward-facing ones that seem to continue the Romantic system: *La esposa del vengador, En el puño de la espada, En el pilar y en la cruz, En el seno de la muerte, La muerte en los labios,* and others. The mere titles of these plays are significant, and they are in fact Romantic in subject, in their striving for effect *(efectismo)*, and in stylistic color. Too often they wring our souls at the expense of all probability. Both incidents and characters are too far from reality. The author slips into melodrama on the slightest pretext, and heaps up extraordinary events and surprising *coups de théatre;* he is too lavish with his murders, his poisons and his daggers; his theater becomes a real massacre.

But this neo-romantic drama is not Echegaray's only string; he has also a thesis drama, a social drama, to be studied in *O locura o santidad* (1877), *Lo que no puede decirse* (1877), *El gran Galeoto* (1881), *Conflicto entre dos deberes* (1882), and *El hijo de don Juan* (1892), which are of the best of this genre and the author's masterpieces.

The first of these, *O locura o santidad,* is an unusual thesis play. The thesis is that real honesty may be mistaken for madness. It is an interesting observation which the author combines with a compelling plot to produce a very effective drama. The thesis is far-fetched, obviously, and the chief character is a fantastic creation, consistent throughout, but rare indeed. Lorenzo, a giant of a man, is finally declared insane, because of his genuine, unswerving honesty. His daughter is the real, though unintended, victim of his determination to do "right" as he saw it, because she is thus kept from marrying the eligible young man she loves. There are some powerful scenes of tragedy and pathos in this prose drama, a lofty tone ever present, classic almost in this respect recalling the atmosphere of the Greek tragedy, spine-tingling, emotional, gripping, though not always logical. Characterization is excellent in this play, normal generally, except for this one romantic, almost grotesque Lorenzo.

More shocking yet to the delicate sensibilities of an 1877 audience must *Lo que no puede decirse* have been. Also a prose drama, in it Echegaray makes use of startling *coups de théatre* of his earlier Romantic dramas (rape and suicide) to prove the thesis that because of the curiosity, moral prejudices, and usual misunderstanding of people in certain situations, the truth cannot be told, lest the telling occasion tragic consequences. He proves his thesis effectively, but the background circumstances and exposition are the products of a too-vivid imagination. Too much, including the turning point in the drama, depends wholly on chance. As in the first play, Echegaray's final scene depends on its heart-rending tableau for much of its effectiveness. The characters are not impressive in this play; all are above average in the artist's gallery of Goyesque portraits, but none is of the stature of Lorenzo.

On the evening of March 19, 1881, there was produced at the Teatro Español, *El gran Galeoto*, Echegaray's masterpiece. This play is undoubtedly the best and most popular of his works and one that will always give the author a place in the dramatic literature of the world. When the play was first produced, it was received with universal applause, and the Spaniards hailed Echegaray as a second Shakespeare. While the work is not that of Shakespeare at his best, it is, nevertheless, one of the best dramatic compositions of the last century.

The curious thesis, which the author fairly well proves, is that it is possible for a mistaken idea to be talked about and repeated often enough, through carelessness and malice, to produce the situation suggested. The plot is assisted in its development by the usual assortment of duels and suspected adultery, the sensational effects Echegaray knew would fill the theater with the excitement-seeking playgoers.

As a work of art, *El gran Galeoto* is also without doubt a drama of real merit. The author's verse has been perfected, there is dramatic unity throughout, and, above all, there is lacking the artificiality and grotesqueness which are found in many of his productions. In some of the scenes of the wonderful play, we find real poetic inspiration.

Conflicto entre dos deberes (1882) is perhaps the most representative of Echegaray's thesis plays. This title gives the essence of most of them, the uncertainty or moral hesitancy encountered in having to choose between two obligations when people must suffer from either choice. The thesis here seems to be that it is of little moral value to fulfill a duty or obligation if, in so doing, one loses his own happiness and destroys that of others. Resorting to the duel, murder, and suicide, Echegaray composed another "hit" for the easily-entertained, not-so-discriminating Madrid audience. This is perhaps the weakest of these five dramas. The sonorous verse and the "emotional" scenes of violence were enough to please the audience, but *Conflicto entre dos deberes* is still melodrama. In his eternal conflicts between duties Echegaray often exaggerates.

The year 1892 may be said to mark the beginning of the Spanish theater's efforts to align itself with the modern theaters of other European countries. Three new plays by as many well-known dramatists appeared in that year: Pérez Galdós's first prose play *Realidad*, *La huelga de hijos* of Enrique Gaspar, and *El hijo de don Juan* by Echegaray. In his play, Echegaray purports to indicate the tragic consequences, in a family, of the father's extramarital sex life. The author shows here the ravages of social disease on a promising young writer, the son of don Juan, ending in his madness. The influence of the Norwegian dramatist Henrik Ibsen has been pointed out. The Echegaray play is symbolic and romantic, really a poignant tragedy, as Echegaray himself said, "a supreme warning to society and the family circle".

With all his romantic tendencies, Echegaray is revealed as typical of the transition period of the nineteenth century, having written many such romantico-historical dramas early in life, then changing to the moral theater as set up by his immediate predecessors in the thesis drama. It is only natural that his second period should reflect certain characteristics of and be influenced by the first. It might be said that a rather farfetched thesis frequently is the starting point in his later dramas (1875-1895). His plays are made absorbing in his lavish use of violence. Characterization is often grotesque, though in several plays, and especially in *El gran Galeoto*, real individuals are to be found. A lofty tone in a kind of other-worldly atmosphere pervades many of his plays. Echegaray is at the same time realistic and strangely romantic. He manages to defend his thesis well enough without recourse to a *raisonneur*. There is great emphasis on staging in his dramas. *Coups de théatre* are employed to a great extent, and these, at the end of acts, are usually accompanied by a slow curtain preceded by a striking tableau. It seems that Echegaray depended on the theatrical effects to imprint indelibly his moral lesson on the minds of the audience.

There is no doubt that the punishment of sin is Echegaray's moral code, and frequently the innocent are punished with the guilty. The moral conflict between duties is found in his dramas, with emphasis, recalling the Siglo de Oro drama, on Love, Honor, and Truth.

The solution of his dramas is often brought about by suicide, and much of the action depends on chance. Needless to say, *vraisemblance* is not an everpresent guest in Echegaray's playhouse.

Tragedy is always the keynote in Echegaray's thesis dramas because, through tragic circumstances, he was able to present more dramatically his unusual theses. The conflict in some plays assumes something of that of ancient Greek tragedy; this is observed in connection with the lofty tone which prevails.

It is generally agreed that Echegaray came under the influence of Ibsen in his later plays, with emphasis on insanity and the coldly philosophical aspect of the Scandinavian drama. But Echegaray's form, manner, and procedure are really quite unique in the drama of the nineteenth century. He started a school, but his followers could not excel their leader.

There is much to recommend in the works of Echegaray. He was the greatest and most popular dramatist of Spain during the last twenty-five years of the nineteenth century. The name of Echegaray will always be mentioned with respect in the annals of dramatic literature.

In addition to the great playwrights already mentioned, there were many others writing in Spain in the nineteenth century, a large percentage of them enjoying considerable fame for their dramatic production. Among the most prolific and of extreme facility was Tomás Rodríguez Rubí (1817-1890). Because of his unusually long period of productivity, almost half a century, beginning in 1840, it is difficult to place him in any one period. His early works reflect the characteristics of Bretón and Vega, and in their day these three were lords of the comic stage. Finally, however, Rubí in some of his best works appears as a progenitor of modern comedy based upon a more realistic study of society; so *El arte de hacer fortuna* and *El gran filón*. He was in this respect an innovator, like Ventura de la Vega, and aided in the transition from Romanticism to the drama of Eguílaz, Ayala, and Echegaray. The chronology and variety of his work, then, makes it seem unwise to try to place him exactly. He has been grouped here with the more important members of a "minor" group of playwrights, but his name in respect to production heads this list.

Characteristics of the Moratinian school appear in his *comedias de costumbres contemporáneas*, and the two plays mentioned approximate in tone and purpose social drama. As can be seen in a study of his works, he had no clearly defined specialty, on the contrary, diversity is one of his marked literary characteristics. Each of these two plays reflects the author's earnest desire to call attention to the need of improvement of *mores*. But his chief purpose was to entertain; his plays are of only "indirecta moralidad".

José Marco y Sanchís (1830-1895) also cultivated the *comedia de costumbres de tendencia moralizador*. Some of his dramatic efforts seem to contain a moral purpose, and *Figuras de cera*, the last of his plays studied here, is a real thesis play, though the thesis is almost improbable, dealing in part, with the problem of education of young girls. In two of the three plays, a *raisonneur* voices the author's opinion on the subject. Unfortunately, the characters were delineated all out of proportion to present his thesis. Marco does not seem to have attained the skill in characterization to be observed in better playwrights. As has been said, the *comedias* of Marco y Sanchís have a moral purpose, are at times graceful and charming, but contain little poesy. His preferred types are men of little character and shallow, excitement-seeking women. Real emotion, feeling, and depth are not to be found in his plays.

The great contribution of José Echegaray to the late nineteenth-century Spanish theater has been indicated. His influence was profound and far-reaching. Indeed, it is generally agreed that he started a school. Among the followers of Echegaray are Eugenio Sellés, Leopoldo Cano y Masas, Enrique Gaspar, Joaquín Dicenta, and Benito Pérez Galdós.

Though Sellés (1844-1926) wrote several successful dramas, none achieved the success of the intriguing triangle play *El nudo gordiano,* the first dramatic plea for adequate divorce laws in Spain. He did not have the same luck with *El cielo y el suelo, Las esculturas de carne,* or *La vida pública,* though each of these has some estimable qualities. In his greatest play, Sellés portrays a tragic case of adultery which was ended only by the murder of the adulteress by her outraged husband. It was for those times a shocking spectacle, though the theme of adultery was certainly not strange to the Spanish theater. As it often was with Echegaray, the Golden Age idea of *pundonor* is important in this drama. Characterization is capably handled, and no *raisonneur* appears, though something of a discussion takes place among the leading characters about the institution of divorce and the many problems to which it might give a happy ending in Spanish society. Most of Sellés's better dramas are "docente y de tesis"; the tone is sometimes definitely Echegarayan; characterization is usually realistic, though a grotesquely-delineated giant, "santo" or "tonto" sometimes appears, as was not infrequent with Echegaray. In his other plays Sellés attacks dueling, the consequences of *pundonor,* apathy, and public or civic service when it destroys, in addition to one's character, the more important life of the family. In the plays studied, the dramatic talent of Sellés is shown to best advantage, but the critics have not dealt kindly with him. He must be relegated to a minor position in the drama of late nineteenth-century Spain.

Leopoldo Cano y Masas (1844-1904), knew, in his turn, some glorious first nights, especially the one when *La pasionaria* was performed; this piece is superior to all his others. In it the author attacks the law and tradition which condemns the fallen woman, the poor girl who has been seduced on promise of marriage, then deserted by her lover. Characterization is mediocre in this play, yet reminiscent of Echegaray in the person of Marcial, the "giant" of the play; he is also the *raisonneur,* preaching against the iniquitous law that protects the adulterer or seducer. The thesis is valid, and the play makes the need of change apparent. *La opinión pública* is a thesis play showing the consequences of this powerful force. *Trata de blancos* is a somewhat antedated money play. The *raisonneur* in this play is a young man; the author thus anticipates the practice of later playwrights, who look toward a brighter future through the youth of the nation.

Enrique Gaspar (1842-1902), who judged the theater of his day with great penetration and clearness of vision, himself wrote for the stage realistic thesis plays of sure aim and excellent style. Notable among these were: *Las circunstancias, La levita, Don Ramón y el señor Ramón, El estómago, La lengua, Lola, Las personas decentes, La huelga de hijos,* and *La eterna cuestión.* They treat the usual things which act as forces for morality or its opposite in everyday life. His characters are usually normal human individuals, often an improvement over those of his predecessors in this group. Gaspar's field of enterprise was more extensive than that of his predecessors. Whereas Tamayo and Ayala had occupied themselves chiefly with the members of the upper middle class, Gaspar steps into the lives of the clerks and petty officials of the lower levels of the bourgeoisie. As in real life, comedy is mixed with tragedy with Gaspar. No serious play of Gaspar's is lacking in comedy, but for the most part his humor is fundamentally a bitter satire. Gaspar was saluted as the standard-bearer of progress in the theater. The *raisonneur* sometimes assists the drama in teaching the moral lesson. Gaspar never failed to present living characters whose collective actions impressed some lesson of social ethics upon the public mind. Gaspar wrote usually in prose, subscribing to that school of *dramaturgos* who believed the language of the street effective on the stage. His playwriting practice was almost the same in all his works. He shocked the native audiences by his unadorned realism and his frank and necessarily brutal presentation of a social problem. Absence of vengeance in his plays left the horror of the vice attacked firmly and, he hoped, perhaps indelibly stamped on the minds of his audience. Gaspar was a sincere crusader. The Spanish people would have profited had they chosen to follow his precepts.

In the second half of the century, Núñez de Arce (1832-1905), the lyric poet, turned playwright for a time, presenting in the

1860's four plays which some critics have called "alta comedia". Of these, two seem to contain the essence of social drama: *Deudas de honra* and *Justicia providencial*. They have a philosophical and moralizing tone which permits them to be classified as that type of social drama established by Tamayo and Ayala. But the drama of social implication was not Núñez de Arce's genre. His plots are unlikely, complicated, completely lacking in *vraisemblance*. Though a moral is much in evidence, the author does not make a happy combination of story and lesson. *Raisonneur* help was needed. The first play has all the characteristics of an Echegaray drama, though it antedated Echegaray's first play by ten years.

Justicia providencial is a drama of "tendencias sociales", as the author himself called it. An improvement over his earlier dramatic efforts, it too is unnecessarily complicated, but characterization shows an improvement. His philosophy was conservative. Though interested in progress, he seeks improvement in social conditions by restoring respect for established traditions.

As the end of the nineteenth century drew near, another devotee of the Echegaray cult was presenting plays of social import of an entirely different type. Joaquín Dicenta (1863-1917), the author of *Los irresponsables, José, El señor feudal,* and *Daniel,* in these plays enlarged considerably the scope of Spanish drama. A new class of people, the proletariat, made its appearance in a new and distinctive manner, not for atmosphere or comic effect, as was the case in the Siglo de Oro, when a *rústico* would appear on stage only to be the butt of cruel jokes. It was with a revolutionary purpose that Dicenta introduced this class, and, not infrequently was this class the very protagonist of the play. This was Dicenta's aim — to advocate improvement of social conditions, even by overthrow of the newly-rich capitalists who were exploiting the proletariat, if this should be necessary.

Aside from his first play, *Los irresponsables,* written in verse, romantic, completely Echegarayan (Echegaray was at the pinnacle of his success at this time), and containing poetic descriptions of pastoral beauties not expected in social drama, all of Dicenta's dramas deal with the proletariat. This first drama was another plea for adequate divorce laws such as Sellés had made with *El nudo gordiano,* but these two plays have different treatment, though both end tragically. All of Dicenta's plays end violently and pessimistically. Not a note of optimism is to be discerned in any of Dicenta's works. The tone is ever gloomy. And Zolaesque naturalism is much in evidence.

The last three plays, all written in prose, center around a factory, a *finca*, and a mine. In each of them an individual representative of the proletariat "rights" a wrong (some form of oppression) by taking violent action against the oppressor, a capitalist, symbolic of Dicenta's purpose. There is much of the romantic to be found in the protagonist of the drama *José*. Indeed, he is a romantic hero in many ways. A comparatively new note, scenes from a prison, appear here, the better to portray the life of the downtrodden. Like Echegaray, Dicenta was *efectista*, and this weakness diminishes the beauty of his dramas. Dicenta's concern for the proletariat links him with dramatists of other countries who used their art to improve the life of workers.

Benito Pérez Galdós (1843-1920), the greatest Spanish novelist of his day, was also an effective social playwright. His first drama, *Realidad*, appeared in 1892. In this play, the author purports to give a realistic treatment of the problem of adultery on a sound, lofty, philosophical and psychological plane. Like the work of his immediate predecessors, this play reflects the Echegaray influence. Indeed Echegaray actually assisted in its staging. But Galdós, the novelist, interfered with Galdós, the playwright, here and elsewhere. The work is diffuse, the author unable to condense it for effective dramatic presentation; and like many of his novels *Realidad* is too long. Though its success was questionable, it indicated that the budding playwright, besides being an innovator had something to say. The solution of the problem is singularly lacking in the expected vengeance theme, and for this reason it received harsh reviews from the traditional press.

In *La loca de la casa* (1893) Galdós's dramatic technique improved. Here he advocates the amalgamation of the good elements of the industrious proletariat with their counterpart among the aristocracy to found a new and better group of people through whose combined efforts Spain could advance and resume its position of importance in the modern world. In this play, Galdós shows his opposition to organized charity and his opinion of duelling as a childish practice. The characters are a little overdrawn for emphasis, and Cruz, the representative of the proletariat, acts also as *raisonneur*. He is a giant of a characterization suggesting again Echegaray's guiding hand. An idiosyncracy of Galdós's becomes apparent here — his tendency to use his characters, and to name them, symbolically.

With *La de San Quintín* (1894), Galdós achieved his first real success as a dramatist. In this play again he advocates fusion of the social classes, giving the best of the proletariat an opportunity to rise through its efforts and ability. A second theme is evident —that true love cannot be blocked by the difference in social classes. Victor, the illegitimate proletarian, acts as *raisonneur*.

Voluntad (1894) is an attack on that failing of Spanish failings, *abulia*. Though lacking in *vraisemblance*, especially in characterization, the play recommends that any country may progress and improve its social conditions by hard work. The will (voluntad) to work is all that is needed. Symbolism is ever in evidence. Some critics declared that the unique philosophy of the play suggests the influence of Ibsen, though Galdós declared that such was not his intention.

In 1896, Galdós presented *Doña Perfecta*, a dramatic version of one of his most controversial novels of the 1870's. In twenty-six years times change even in Spain, and the author's anticlericalism was said to have been unjustified at the time the play was presented, though few of the intellectual progressives denied its practicality or need in 1876, and the play apparently had little influence toward changing the powerful hold the Spanish Jesuits and other religious groups have on the bulk of the Spanish people. This play is Galdós's most symbolical effort. Each of the four leading roles represents definite attitudes of Spanish society. The author's ideas on clericalism take human form in the effective characterization of the obscurantist priest, don Inocencio. Doña Perfecta represents arch-conservatism in close alliance with the church. The pitiful Rosario is Spain herself, helpless in the clutches of these forces. Pepe Rey, her novio, is the cosmopolitan personification of progress. This is one of Galdós's best and most profound plays.

The play which Galdós and his ever-growing group of admirers thought epoch-making was *Electra* (1901). Though not his best play, its presentation was the occasion for near rioting, against which the mayor of Madrid was forced to take measures. *Electra* is another symbolic drama in which Galdós voices his antipathy toward monastery-founding and clericalism. This play had a great effect on the public. It has been discussed pro and con in Spain ever since. His characterization-ability, as well as his dramatic ingenuity, had so much improved by this time that Galdós was hailed as a new Shakespeare.

El abuelo (1904) marks the highest attainment of Galdós's dramatic art. This drama, first a dialogued novel, had all the appealing elements necessary for an interesting play. A sympathetic old man, the Conde de Albrit, representing the old regime, standing for the best traditions of the past, discovers in Dolly, the illegitimate daughter of his son's wife, virtues unsuspected among those who are not of noble blood. Galdós thus points out again the potentialities of the lower economic levels of society.

In the works of Pérez Galdós are discerned the sound ideas of this genius for the betterment of life in general and everywhere, not only in Spain. This novelist-playwright was profoundly concerned for his own country's fate and identifies himself with the youth of Spain as her hope for the future. It is to be lamented that this polygraph did not essay the field of the drama earlier in his long and useful literary life, that he might have developed his dramatic skills and have kept on writing provocative dramas. It seems doubtless that his influence would have been felt to an even greater extent. But Galdós, like Enrique Gaspar, was ahead of his time. His concept of the drama was beyond the reach of the average intelligence.

In conclusion, in this book an attempt has been made to study the various types of social problems in Spain in the nineteenth century as they were presented in the drama. Early in the century the theme for several playwrights on frequent occasions was abuse of authority as seen in the parent-children or guardian-children relationship. Later the topics became more general as with the socio-moral problem of the money-question providing material for leading dramatists of the third quarter of the century. As the social theater developed, more attention was drawn to the need for adequate divorce laws in Spain. Near the end of the century, with the arrival of a new protagonist to the theater, the proletariat, violence leading to the overthrow of the capitalistic

CONCLUSIONS

system was advocated by Dicenta as the remedy for the sufferings of that economic group. And, finally, a general solution to Spain's social problems was offered by Pérez Galdós, namely fusion of the social classes, through which Spain might hope to improve her social conditions. That Galdós did not begin writing for the stage earlier and that he might have lived to write more in the field of social drama is to be regretted. With his plays Spanish social drama reached the twentieth century.

BIBLIOGRAPHY

GENERAL

ADAMS, NICHOLAS B., *The Heritage of Spain*, New York, 1943.
ALTAMIRA, RAFAEL, AND MUNA LEE, *A History of Spain*, New York, 1949.
ASENSIO, CALVO, *El teatro hispano-lusitano en el siglo XIX*, Madrid, 1875.
BELL, AUBREY F. G., *Castilian Literature*, Oxford University Press, 1938.
BLANCO GARCÍA, P. FRANCISCO, *La literatura española en el siglo XIX*, 3 vols., Madrid, 1909-1912.
BOGGS, R. S., *Outline History of Spanish Literature*, New York, 1937.
CEJADOR Y FRAUCA, JULIO, *Historia de la lengua y literatura castellana*, 13 vols., 1915-1920.
CHAPMAN, C. E., *A History of Spain*, New York, 1918.
COTARELO Y MORI, EMILIO, *Estudios de historia literaria de España*, Madrid, 1901.
DES GRANGES, CH.-M., *Histoire illustrée de la literature française*, Paris, 1947.
DÍAZ DE ESCOVAR, NARCISO AND FRANCISCO DE P. LASSO DE LA VEGA, *Historia del teatro español*, 2 vols., Barcelona, 1924.
ESPASA-CALPE, *Enciclopedia universal ilustrada*, Barcelona, 81 vols., 1912-1935.
GAYLEY, C. M., *The Classic Myths*, New York, 1893.
HURTADO, JUAN Y ÁNGEL GONZÁLEZ PALENCIA, *Historia de la literatura española*, Madrid, 1943.
LAROUSSE, *Nuevo pequeño Larousse ilustrado*, Paris, 1952.
LATIMER, E. W., *Spain in the Nineteenth Century*, Chicago, 1897.
MADARIAGA, SALVADOR DE, *Spain*, London, 1942.
MÉRIMÉE, ERNEST AND MORLEY, S. G., *A History of Spanish Literature*, New York, 1930.
NITZE, W. A., AND E. P. DARGAN, *A History of French Literature*, New York, 1938.
Teatro Español Series, Bound Collection of Nineteenth Century plays, 606 vols., at the University of North Carolina Library, Chapel Hill, N. C.
VALBUENA-PRAT, ÁNGEL, *Historia de la literatura española*, 2 vols., Barcelona, 1946.

SPECIFIC

ALARCÓN Y MENDOZA, JUAN RUIZ DE, *La verdad sospechosa*.
ALPERN, H., AND J. MARTEL, *Diez comedias del siglo de oro*, New York, 1939.

BERKOWITZ, H. C., *Galdós, Spanish Liberal Crusader*, University of Wisconsin Press, 1948.
CASALDUERO, J., *Vida y obra de Galdós*, Buenos Aires, 1943.
ESPINOSA, AURELIO M., *Ayala: Consuelo*, New York, 1911.
ESPINOSA, AURELIO M., *Echegaray: El gran Galeoto*, New York, 1918.
GAMERO, E. G., *Galdós y su obra*, Madrid, 1935.
GRANDGENT, C. H., *La Divina Commedia de Dante Alighieri*, New York, 1933.
GREGERSEN, HALFDAN, *Ibsen and Spain*, Harvard University Press, 1936.
HARRY, P., AND A. DE SALVIO, *Tamayo: Lo positivo*, New York, 1908.
HERNÁNDEZ, GUSTAVO RENÉ, *The Dramatic Works of Enrique Gaspar*, M. A. thesis, University of North Carolina, 1944.
HERNÁNDEZ, PASCUAL, *Comedias de Moratín*, Paris, 1881.
KIRSCHENBAUM, LEO, *Enrique Gaspar and The Social Drama in Spain*, University of California Press, 1944.
LESLIE, JOHN KENNETH, *Ventura de la Vega and The Spanish Theatre (1820-1865)*, Princeton, 1940.
LYNCH, H., AND E. R. HUNT, *The Great Galeoto* (by José Echegaray), New York, 1914.
MOORE, JOHN A., *The Dramatic Works of Luis de Eguílaz* (UNC Master's Thesis). Chapel Hill, N. C. 1948.
NÚÑEZ DE ARCE, GASPAR, *Obras dramáticas*, Madrid, 1879.
OLMET, LUIS ANTÓN DE, AND ARTURO GARCÍA CARRAFA, *Los grandes españoles: Galdós*, Madrid, 1912.
PEERS, E. ALLISON, *A History of the Romantic Movement in Spain*, Cambridge, 1940.
RENNERT, H. A., *The Spanish Stage in the Time of Lope de Vega*, New York, 1909.
SEAY, H. W., *The Dramatic works of Gaspar Núñez de Arce*, M. A. thesis University of North Carolina, 1953.
SHIELDS, A. K., *Adelardo López de Ayala and The Spanish Stage*, M. A. thesis University of North Carolina, 1930.
VENTURA DE LA VEGA, *Obras escogidas de*, 2 vols., Barcelona, 1894.
YXART Y MORAGAS, JOSÉ, *El arte escénico en España*, 2 vols., Barcelona, 1894-1896.

The Department of Romance Studies Digital Arts and Collaboration Lab at the University of North Carolina at Chapel Hill is proud to support the digitization of the North Carolina Studies in the Romance Languages and Literatures series.